P9-DEO-909

school success for kids with Asperger's Syndrome

school success for kids with

Asperger's Syndrome

Stephan M. Silverman, Ph.D., & Rich Weinfeld

PRUFROCK PRESS INC.
WACO, TEXAS

Library of Congress Cataloging-in-Publication Data

Silverman, Stephan, 1942–
School success for kids with Asperger's syndrome / Stephan Silverman & Rich Weinfeld.
p. cm.
Includes bibliographical references.
ISBN-13: 978-1-59363-215-1 (pbk.)
ISBN-10: 1-59363-215-0
1. Asperger's syndrome—Patients—Education. 2. Autistic children—Education. 3. Academic achievement. I. Weinfeld, Rich, 1953– II. Title.
LC4717.S55 2007
371.94—dc22
2007007579

Edited by Lacy Elwood
Editorial Assistant: Kate Sepanski
Cover and Layout Design by Marjorie Parker

ISBN-13: 978-1-59363-215-1
ISBN-10: 1-59363-215-0

Printed in the United States of America.

Prufrock Press Inc.
P.O. Box 8813
Waco, TX 76714-8813
Phone: (800) 998-2208
Fax: (800) 240-0333
http://www.prufrock.com

Dedication

To our parents, Milton and Judith Silverman and Charles and Irene Weinfeld, who gave us the gift of the love of learning and always held high expectations for each of us.

We also would like to dedicate this book to our wives, Karin Silverman and Sara Shelley, in appreciation of their love, support, and patience that made this project possible.

Contents

Introduction xi

chapter 1
What Is Asperger's Syndrome? 1

chapter 2
How Might AS Appear to a Parent? 13

chapter 3
Recognizing and Diagnosing AS 27

chapter 4
Additional Aspects of AS 57

chapter 5
Best Practices in School 71

chapter 6
Strategies and Interventions That Work in the Classroom 81

chapter 7
Working With the School System: Options for Students With AS 125

chapter 8
Best Practices for Parenting and Raising Kids With AS 147

chapter 9
Other Experiences: College, Work, and Independent Living 167

chapter 10
School Success for Kids With AS 175

References 181

Appendix A 197

Appendix B 203

Appendix C 204

Appendix D 210

Appendix E 215

Appendix F 216

About the Authors 221

Acknowledgements

We would like to acknowledge Drs. Brenda Smith Myles and Dan Shapiro for their insightful reviews of parts of this book. We would also like to express our gratitude to our editor, Lacy Elwood.

We also would like to acknowledge the many families we have worked with, the school administrators and teachers we have had the privilege to collaborate with, and finally, the students with AS themselves, who provide us with daily inspiration.

Introduction

STANLEY, 13, was sitting at the dinner table across from his grandfather. The table had been cleared and the family had moved to the den to watch a football game. As usual on such evenings, Grandpa engaged Stanley in his favorite topic of interest—World War II history. Grandpa served in the infantry in Europe and was trying to get a word in edgewise from his memory about a particular campaign, but Stanley was going on and on about the very battle in which Grandpa fought. Finally, Grandpa interrupted Stanley to correct a factual detail. Apparently, Stanley had incorrectly identified the name of the commanding officer on a specific day of the conflict. Even though he took part in the battle, Grandpa's memory was shaky. He thought he was right. Stanley went to his room and pulled out a reference book. Stanley was right! There didn't seem to be anything Stanley didn't know about the war. He continued to reel off fact after fact in a determined, but emotionless, monotone, hardly looking toward his grandfather's face the whole time. Grandpa wanted to share stories of the friends he made and lost in the war, the emotions he felt, and the human drama he experienced, but Stanley seemed only interested in tactical facts and the names of generals. Grandpa wasn't sure that what he thought, knew, or remembered about the war really mattered to Stanley. They weren't really connecting. Stanley, like thousands of other children, has Asperger's syndrome (AS), a form of autism.

This book is written for parents, educators, and other professionals who are concerned with providing an education to children like Stanley. It focuses on providing practical strategies that can be used by parents and classroom teachers, and summarizes relevant research in the ever-expanding field of the education of students with Asperger's syndrome. Because a detailed review of research is beyond the scope of this book, we encourage interested readers to refer to the works of the leaders in this field, including Drs. Hans Asperger, Tony Attwood, Simon Baron-Cohen, Mohammad Ghaziuddin, Christopher Gillberg, Ami Klin, Brenda Smith Myles, Sally Ozonoff, Michael Powers, Fred R. Volkmar, and Lorna Wing. If we have omitted the recognition of other pivotal individuals in this area of research and application of knowledge, we apologize. Very few researchers have directly addressed the wide variety of issues involved in general and special education for students with AS. A few notable exceptions in the literature are Drs. Attwood, Ozonoff, Baron-Cohen, Klin, Myles, and Volkmar. Their work, along with that of others, will be discussed briefly in relation to the education of students with Asperger's syndrome in the chapters that follow.

Asperger's syndrome, which we often will refer to as AS, should be recognized as early as possible in the developing child. Not only do we hope that the diagnosis will be applied as early as possible and with accuracy, but we hope that the strengths of each child with AS can be found and supported in the educational environment. The educational experience for children like Stanley should support their zeal and intellectual ability so that learning can be as joyful and productive as the experience is for other children. Children are all born wanting to learn, and the experience of learning should be a happy one—starting with early development until the young person becomes a productive member of society. Because AS is an autistic spectrum disorder, not just a developmental difference or aggregate of eccentricities, children with AS will, at some time in their educational careers, need special approaches to education to learn the facts and skills they are incapable of accessing because of their disability. Special education may not be required in every subject area and skill domain. To whatever extent possible, the child with AS should have learning experiences that work for more typically developing children, as long as he or she is deriving meaningful benefit from these learning opportunities and is able to access the curriculum.

To whatever extent possible, the child with AS should have learning experiences that work for more typically developing children, as long as he or she is deriving meaningful benefit from these learning opportunities and is able to access the curriculum.

The focus of this book is not only to accept and affirm the humanity of children with AS and aid them in obtaining their right to an education that is consistent with typical development, but also to "fill in the gaps" where their special needs hamper their ability to access instruction and progress in knowledge. As for children with any disability, the definition of a disability implies the need for additional support in educational areas. However, there is a set of instructional strategies and targeted skill areas beyond the curriculum that require emphasis in order for children with AS to function in a complex and competitive world. We will discuss these strategies and skill areas later in the book.

This book is about the special opportunities to enhance learning for children with AS in accommodating for and instructing in their areas of need, while celebrating and nurturing their special skills. We hope to provide functional guidelines for teachers who have these children in their charge. The first half of this book is a general survey of AS with an attempt to highlight critical issues in diagnosis, treatment, and education. Keep in mind as you are reading this book that not all of the information available on AS could be included in a short reference book like this one. We are at an early point in the history of this field and at the beginning of an explosion of critically important new research on AS. You will want to seek out other resources as you begin to understand your child's disorder, including books, centers of study, and Web sites. Many such resources are listed in Appendix A. The second half of the book focuses entirely on interventions for children and young adults with AS. These include best practices for working with these students in the classroom, as well as tips for parents in how to navigate the school system to provide the best fit for their child and advice for supporting their child's learning at home. Every child is unique, and therefore, has different needs in and out of the classroom. Some of our suggestions may help more than others, but we hope you find something in this book that you can take to your child's teacher or that you can use in your own classroom with your AS students. We also provide a menu of placement and instructional options to think about as you work with the educational system.

Although there is no cure for AS, this book hopes to provide some preventative interventions and early supports to circumvent long-term effects of the condition. We hope this book helps to educationally support each child in reaching his or her potential and having a successful educational experience. At present, we are on the brink of discovery of pivotal information, especially in the areas of genetics and neurology. When the genetic code for AS has been identified and when emerging techniques in brain imaging have focused on specific areas of weakness or malfunction, we will have come a long way toward securing our knowledge about the brain/behavior relationships that drive educational strategies for children with AS. Today, educators and parents need to work with what information we have in making practical and effective daily decisions. We hope this book will help you help the child in your life with AS succeed in school and beyond.

chapter 1

What Is Asperger's Syndrome?

BEING eccentric or unusual has become increasingly more acceptable. From the awkwardly entertaining lead character in the movie *Napoleon Dynamite*, to the increasing appearance of bookish personalities in TV shows and ads, we are becoming more comfortable with members of our community who were seen in recent times as merely odd. Recently, the word *geek*, initially a derogatory term, has become a humorous, culturally descriptive term for persons who are far more interested intellectually in technical data and activities than they are skilled in working with people. Now there are computer consultation groups and individuals who rent out their services, such as Best Buy's "Geek Squad."

Pictured wearing pocket protectors and heavy horn-rimmed glasses, these same people were called "nerds" just one or two decades previously. When technology was somewhat less sophisticated, these same individuals sported slide rules in leather pouches on their belts. This image of the socially inept "techie" refers to a continuum of persons who lack the ability to read social cues or manage complex relationships, including the complex Western game of dating.

More recently, it has been suggested that social skill deficits are more than a difference or an eccentricity—they can fall into a disability classification requiring special supports. This occurs when the so-called "geekiness" shares characteristics of a form of autism called Asperger's syndrome. In brief, AS is described as a condition thought to lie on the autistic spectrum and characterized by poor social reciprocity and circumscribed technical interests, despite seemingly normal intelligence and language skills. Although we will frequently refer to AS falling on an autistic spectrum, there is disagreement in the field about whether these disabilities truly occur on a continuum. For example, researchers Klin, Volkmar, and Sparrow (2000) feel that many of the forms of autism, including AS, may be distinct entities. Hans Asperger, the Viennese psychiatrist for whom the syndrome was named, saw this group as quite a distinct genetic set of "little professors" (Asperger, 1944).

History of AS

In order to better understand children with AS, it's helpful to know some of the history behind the discovery of Asperger's as a disorder and the subsequent research and treatment that has followed. The term *autism* was first used by Dr. Eugen Bleuler (1857–1939) to identify extreme egocentrism or a shutting off of relations between the individual and others. The discovery of the group of people we now consider as having AS is attributed to Hans Asperger (1906–1980), who, after working with hundreds of children, reported on a study of four subjects displaying AS characteristics, ages 6 to 11, in Vienna in 1944. In the four boys he studied, Asperger identified a pattern of behavior and abilities that he originally called "autistic personality disorders in childhood," and later referred to as "autistic psychopathy," meaning "self-personality disease." Autistic psychopathy was for Asperger a constitutionally given personality type. He noted that almost all of the children were boys and all had at least one parent, usually the father, with a similar, but less extreme, set of traits. Asperger's (1944) observed the following traits: empathy, little ability to form friendships, conversation that was one-sided, intense absorption in a special interest, and clumsy physical movements.

Asperger developed a strengths model of the children, whom he identified in this group as having "autistic psychopathy" (Frith, 1991). He deemphasized their weaknesses, believing that their strengths would carry into adulthood. One example he noted was a child named Fritz V. True to Asperger's expectations, Fritz did manifest his strengths into adulthood and became a professor of astronomy, solving an error in Newton's work that Fritz first had discovered as a child. Asperger was a pioneer in the education of his subjects, opening a school for this group of children near the end of World War II. Sadly, the school was bombed and demolished. This may have contributed to further delays in the transfer of knowledge from Asperger's findings to the West, as much of his work was destroyed.

It has been speculated that Asperger may have possessed aspects of the condition later named after him by Lorna Wing, a British researcher. He himself was an isolated child who found it difficult to make friends. He had a seemingly obsessive interest in an Austrian poet, and he repeatedly recited passages from the poet's works to his classmates, who did not share his enthusiasm on the material.

Asperger wrote in German and his work was not frequently translated into other languages. It was not until the publication of "Asperger's Syndrome: A Clinical Account" in 1981 by Wing in the journal *Psychological Medicine* that Asperger received enduring recognition. Wing's study of 35 individuals aged 5–35 introduced Asperger's work to the English-speaking world. In her paper, Wing dropped the term autistic psychopathy, because it was seen as stigmatizing and suggestive of voluntary antisocial actions in the individuals described by the label. In 1991, Asperger's work was translated into English 47 years after his original publication.

Dr. Leo Kanner, often referred to as the father of child psychiatry, was working with similar children at Johns Hopkins University in Baltimore, MD, around the same time Asperger was conducting his study. Kanner and Asperger initially had no knowledge of each other and, when they did, they corresponded briefly, but believed that they were working with two very different kinds of children. Kanner's subjects were more severe, with a broader range of symptoms, and often were less intelligent than those children described by Asperger. Kanner first described the children he was working with as having "autistic disturbances of affective contact" (1943), which he later referred to as *early infantile autism* (Kanner & Eisenberg, 1956). As mentioned earlier, AS and autism now are considered to be related on a severity spectrum or, at least, they share functional similarities. This continuum has only been accepted in general thinking in the last decade. Previously, Kanner placed autism within the categories of schizophrenia, and other psychoanalysts most frequently attributed the cause, although unknown, to "refrigerator" mothers (parents who appeared to lack the ability to demonstrate affection to their children and who may have, consciously or unconsciously, been rejecting them). During this time, parents not only had to adjust to the challenge of rearing an autistic child, they also were made to feel guilty that their child's disabilities were the result of poor parenting.

Autism was thought to be an emotional disturbance related to schizophrenia or a form of mental retardation, instead of the varieties of congenital neurological atypicality it is considered to be today. Whereas Kanner's work became accepted internationally, much of the research on AS that followed took place in Great Britain and Scandinavia.

AS has only been classified as a form of autism in the mental health practitioner's guidebook, the American Psychiatric Association's *Diagnostic and Statistical Manual (DSM-IV)*, since the manual's fourth edition in 1994. AS was not accepted as a specific classification of autism until the 1990s (Safran, 2001), whereas autism as a group of conditions was recognized in the DSM system in 1980. An international classification for AS was established in 1992 by the International Classification of Diseases (ICD; World Health Organization 2006).

AS has been the subject of research outside of the United States for about 20 years and is only recently emerging in interest in the U.S. Therefore, instructional processes for children with this disorder are only recently being developed and refined. Interest in AS has grown as schools have experienced an influx of children who appear to be on the autism spectrum. Unlike the range of clinical syndromes, many school districts only have one special education eligibility classification available for autistic spectrum disorder.

The Incidence of AS

Recently, the Centers for Disease Control and Prevention (CDC; n.d.) reported a dramatic increase in the incidence rate of autistic spectrum disorders, which included AS. As the CDC reported on its Web site, approximately one in every 150 children in the United States has autism or a closely related disorder—a figure higher than most recent estimates. The new estimates do not necessarily mean that autism is on the rise, because the criteria and definitions used were not the same as those used in the past. Fourteen U.S. states were surveyed in the CDC study. If extrapolated to 50 states, the total number of children currently with autism would be approximately 560,000 nationwide. This would make autism an urgent public health issue and a major concern, as reported by Dr. Yeargin-Allsopp, chief of the developmental disabilities branch of the CDC (CDC, n.d.). This would highly influence the attention received by parents and other advocates for services to children with autism.

The states studied included all or part of Alabama, Arizona, Arkansas, Colorado, Georgia, Maryland, Missouri, New Jersey, North Carolina, Pennsylvania, South Carolina, Utah, West Virginia, and Wisconsin. The prevalence of autism was similar in most of the states surveyed, with two exceptions. The prevalence was lowest in Alabama, at 1 in 300, and highest in New Jersey, at about 1 in 100 (CDC, n.d.). Dr. Catherine Rice, the CDC researcher who led the study, reported that it was likely that the Alabama number was an underestimate, because the researchers did not have access to school records in that state. The higher rate in New Jersey may reflect other differences, experts said, including a higher level of awareness and wider availability of services in communities and schools.

The results are the first to come out of the CDC's Autism and Developmental Disabilities Monitoring Network, launched in 2000. This program aims to get the most accurate statistics possible on the prevalence of autistic behaviors by collecting information on thousands of children from schools, medical clinics, and social service providers.

Past estimates have varied because there is no simple test to provide a definitive diagnosis and because the behavioral measures used to define autism spectrum disorders have changed over time. The survey looked at records of 8-year-olds, the age by which the vast majority of autistic children have been diagnosed. The new numbers may not reflect the true incidence of autism, because they are derived not from clinical exams but from descriptive reports provided by teachers and others, which were reviewed by experts for key words that suggested a diagnosis of autism, AS, or a related disorder. The CDC currently is comparing selected survey cases with data collected from actual clinical examinations to test the accuracy and validity of the survey's results.

Autism advocates now have increased support for their insistence that the U.S. Congress fund the Combating Autism Act that was passed in December of 2006, which authorized the release of $925 million in research and other funds over 5 years.

Two of the most prominent questions surrounding AS at this time are: "What are the most accurate current statistics on the actual incidence of AS in the population?" and "Is there really a rise in the disorder's occurrence and, if so, why?" It is possible that, to a large extent, the new dramatic numbers from the CDC represent the influx of students with AS or AS-like disorders in the school population.

Previously, estimates of the number of persons with AS in the general population have ranged from 1 in 10,000 to 48 in 10,000 (Kadesjo, Gillberg, & Hagberg, 1999). In 2003, Fombonne reported a review of 32 studies of pervasive developmental disorders (PDD), also on the autism spectrum, published between 1966 and 2001. Surveys at that time suggested that a rate of 30 in 10,000 was an accurate estimate of all forms of PDD, but more recent surveys suggest it might be higher. A report in the *Journal of Autism and Developmental Disorders* found that in the U.S., the diagnosis of autistic spectrum disorders increased from 4–5 children per 10,000 in the

. . . the diagnosis of autistic spectrum disorders increased from 4–5 children per 10,000 in the 1980s to 30–60 children per 10,000 in the 1990s, an almost 10-fold increase during the course of a decade (Fombonne, 2003).

1980s to 30–60 children per 10,000 in the 1990s, an almost 10-fold increase during the course of a decade (Fombonne, 2003).

Lauritsen, Pedersen, & Mortensen (2004) estimated the annual and age-specific prevalence and incidence rates of childhood autism, atypical autism, AS, and pervasive developmental disorder not otherwise specified (PDD-NOS) in Denmark during the period of 1971–2000 in children younger than 10 years from the Danish Psychiatric Central Register. A total of 2.4 million children younger than 10 years were followed and 2,061 cases were identified. The annual incidence rate per 10,000 children younger than 10 years was 2.0 for childhood autism, 0.7 for atypical autism, 1.4 for AS, and 3.0 for PDD-NOS in 2000. Lauritsen and colleagues calculated a corrected prevalence of childhood autism at 11.8, atypical autism at 3.3, AS at 4.7, and PDD-NOS at 14.6 per 10,000 children younger than 10 years on January 1, 2001. Lauritsen and colleagues also found that the estimated prevalence of the PDDs studied was probably underestimated. Furthermore, the increasing prevalence and incidence rates during the 1990s may well be explained by changes in the registration procedures and more awareness of the disorders, although a true increase in the incidence could not be ruled out. If these numbers are correct, then the growth of this diagnosis has been quite substantial. More recently, Fombonne and Tidmarsh (2003) estimated that autism occurs in about 10 in 10,000 children and AS occurs in about 2 in 10,000.

Speculation has spread through the popular press about an "epidemic" of autism and, specifically, AS. However, the meaning of the word *epidemic* seems to have been lost, initially suggesting a communicable disease or something contagious. It is clear from current research that AS is not only being more accurately identified (as are all forms of autism), but also that there does appear to be an increase in incidence of the disorder, although it is not an epidemic in the sense of malaria or polio. Certainly, increased ability to make classification decisions (whether those are right or wrong) have resulted in an increased incidence rate. Rita S. Eagle (2004) expressed her concern over the fact that the autism diagnosis, in general, has been stretched to include an "ever-widening range of clinical presentations, not just among children with limited cognitive resources, but among children with normal or above average intelligence as well" (pp. 87–88).

Articles have been written about population centers where high-tech communities have arisen and where "geeks" marry "geeks," emphasizing that Asperger's is a genetic disorder. Dr. Simon Baron-Cohen is another individual who has hypothesized that people with systemizing brains are finding each other and creating a genetic predisposition toward producing higher rates of AS in their offspring (Morton, 2001). It is true that, more than most other forms of autism, AS is thought to be caused by genetic factors. Other causes for autistic disorders are being explored and include toxicity theories, or the possibility that agents in immunizations may have a causal link to autism. However, these potential toxins and others in the environment thus far have not been conclusively linked to AS. Regardless of the cause, there clearly has been a dramatic increase in persons identified with AS. This has caused school systems to adjust rapidly to implement effective supports and interventions for these students. This is taking place despite disagreements among leading researchers and confusion by educators as to what constitutes the disorder and how it should be measured and addressed academically.

Clinical Versus Educational Classification

Because of the rise in interest in autism, and AS in particular, we must guard against overinclusion in our classification. Not every exceptionally gifted person and not every socially inept person has AS. It has been hypothesized that many creative people, including Albert Einstein and Hans Asperger may have had AS, when in fact these individuals simply may have been brilliant persons with great passion toward solving important problems and lesser skills or interest in negotiating social niceties or complexities. A profound interest or passion in a topic or activity does not in itself qualify one as disabled. In her lectures, Temple Grandin, an accomplished scientist, author, professor, and internationally known spokesperson for persons with AS, who has come to personally understand and overcome many of the challenges of this disorder, poses the question about what a great loss we would have experienced if Thomas Edison were chatting away constantly in social activities instead of persevering in inventing many of our modern conveniences.

Some programs for children with AS are simply ways of isolating and protecting children who are very bright with poor social skills but not autistic. It is important to note that children with high cognitive ability and poor social skills must meet some eligibility criteria where there is a measurable negative educational impact of their weaknesses before they actually are considered disabled.

Separate from a clinical diagnosis, students must be identified with an educational disability in order to qualify for special education services. This identification is governed by federal law in the Individuals with Disabilities Education Act (IDEA) of 1990, which was revised in 1997 and 2004. This law and its ramifications will be discussed in detail in Chapter 7.

It requires considerable expertise, however, to make a diagnosis and to distinguish AS from other similar symptom profiles. Parents, pediatricians, and early childhood educators find it difficult in the early developmental period to accurately integrate their observations of the developing child into a crystal clear classification.

When, however, are the "little professors" more than just intellectually top-heavy and when are they disabled? When the intense interests of the individual become obsessive and nonfunctional and social interaction with others is diminished to the point of little practical effectiveness, the observer may be looking at a form of autism. The critical and pivotal element is the lack of interest or ability to form satisfactory relationships, to demonstrate attachment with others, or to engage in the rich interplay of language and emotional communication valued in our modern society. When social abilities are impaired to this extent, the individual finds himself without the basic skills of functional communication needed to adapt flexible responses for the purpose of survival in the world of school, work, and independent living. AS, as classified by psychiatric and psychological criteria, is more than a relative strength in some technical skills and mild to moderate ineptness in social exchange. It is a meaningful liability in a society. The passion for a given topic in people with AS is sometimes accompanied by obsession with data no one can use or care about and/or an inability to effectively use this enthusiasm and data functionally in a way that serves society. The problem is determining at what point the disconnect between people becomes autistic. It is important to note that it is our goal as advocates to hold high the hopes that individuals with AS will find functional roles as employees and citizens in our society. This requires a strengths-based model and emphasis. Temple Grandin has expressed her concern that intellectually gifted children are being denied opportunities because they are being labeled with either Asperger's or high-functioning autism. She notes that in years past, when a child was found with a very high IQ, the strength was celebrated before the weaknesses were labeled (Grandin, 2001).

When the intense interests of the individual become obsessive and nonfunctional and social interaction with others is diminished to the point of little practical effectiveness, the observer may be looking at a form of autism.

The few studies of adults with this disorder suggest that, for an unfortunately high percentage of people with AS, the quality of life in independent living is marginal and the ability to attain and maintain employment does not paint an optimistic picture without early identification, preventative and supportive education, and community resources. Previously, many unidentified persons with AS were thought to be schizophrenic. Their frustration with negotiating the complex world of social relationships frequently resulted in unemployment and dependent living, with secondary consequences of mental illness and even bouts with the law. The next chapter will discuss the diagnosis of AS in more detail.

chapter 2

How Might AS Appear to a Parent?

AT first, Jack's parents were so excited and proud. He was reading books before the age of 4. It was clear he was a chip off the old block, as bright as his parents, one a Yale graduate and one a Columbia graduate. It was true that he was a little clumsy and his speech was a little delayed, but initially his parents could focus on how incredibly bright he appeared. But, over time his talent and interest in reading became another area of concern. Reading was all he wanted to do. As the other children played with one another, he was still off to the side with his books. In preschool, his problems interacting socially quickly became evident. Jack was either uninterested in the other kids or when he did want someone's attention, he was more likely to push them than to speak to them. When his teachers would try to engage him, he would not make eye contact with them. The feeling of pride and expectation that his parents had initially felt was now being replaced by doubt and fear.

There are many aspects of the developing child that emerge as challenges for parents. Certainly, there are some features in your child's early development that may concern you as parents. In this chapter, we hope to emphasize pivotal developmental concerns that may arise.

Eye Contact

A child with AS may exhibit less eye contact with you and others than expected, and he or she may not read faces for cues about feelings or consequences. This lack of connectivity is often felt in an intangible way, especially by caregivers. We anticipate with open hearts the child who will "give back" our attention. However, in kids with AS, there may be very little variation in expressions of emotions and little joy in playing interactive baby games. The arrival of the child's social smile may occur later and infrequently.

Sensory and Motor Development

There is significant data to suggest that many children with AS frequently show a very exaggerated response to loud noises such as thunder or unexpected sounds. In addition, your child may show hyperresponsiveness to unexpected experiences in general, because a core attribute of AS is sensorimotor dysfunction. Motor clumsiness is often significant. Very few highly athletic children are found in the AS population. They may display some exquisitely developed skills such as mastery of a musical instrument, but rarely do they display general gross motor precocity. They are often awkward in tasks requiring balance and coordination. They are often late to handle a pencil comfortably, catch a ball, ride a bike, or use playground equipment effectively. They often display hypotonia, a generalized muscular weakness that affects posture, movement, strength, and coordination. Children with AS also may display tactile defensiveness; in other words, they may avoid touch, warmth, and hugs. For these reasons, occupational and physical therapies are among the very earliest interventions that should be employed along with speech/language therapy, the most frequently employed early intervention.

Teitelbaum and colleagues (2004) at the University of Florida have identified motor measures of the early developing smile, and postural and other motor movements that they feel demonstrate the possibility of identifying AS in infancy. Teitelbaum's group used a notation system for movements (called the Eshkol-Wachman movement notation) in the attempt to find diagnostic clues about AS early in life. They present evidence that abnormal movement patterns can be detected in AS in infancy. This finding suggests that AS can be diagnosed very early, independent of the presence of language. As shown by the group in earlier studies, almost all of the movement disturbances in autism can be interpreted as infantile reflexes "gone astray." In other words, some reflexes are not inhibited at the appropriate age in development, whereas others fail to appear when they should. This phenomenon appears to apply to AS, as well. Based on preliminary results, a simple test using one such reflex is proposed for the early detection of a subgroup of children with AS or autism. What parents often see, however, are late-developing, immature, and awkward visual-motor skills.

Attachment

The historically important work of Lorna Wing (1981) has suggested that delays and atypicalities related to AS are observable in the first 2 years of life. Some babies with AS show less-than-expected interest and pleasure in other people. Infants with AS may share interests and activities less and may even babble less than other infants. Your baby may seem less interested in communicating through sounds or physical gestures, and his speech may be delayed to some extent or robotically copied from books or TV shows. Wing points out that not all children with AS talk before they walk and not all children with AS are bright. She also notes that young children with AS seem to display limitations in imagination and pretend play, or they employ play themes that are limited and repetitive. Wing also notes that about 20% of the AS population is female. Today, it is clearly accepted that there are 1 in 4 or 1 in 5 girls in the AS population, and that the majority of children with AS are boys. It is important to note that, in many clinical populations involving learning disabilities and differences, that the ratio of boys to girls is higher.

Today, it is clearly accepted that there are 1 in 4 or 1 in 5 girls in the AS population, and that the majority of children with AS are boys.

Children with AS tend to display better attachment to parents than children with more severe forms of classical autism. However, you may notice that despite your child's bonding with you, she still has difficulty connecting with her peers. Later in childhood, she may be more likely to engage in conversation (although this often is one-way conversation) with you and other adults than with her peers.

Perseveration

Almost all children with any form of autism tend to repeat behaviors, an action referred to as *stereotypic behaviors* or *perseveration*. Your child may stare at objects or repeat behaviors that seem to have no purpose for hours at a time. This can be seen in the "flapping" of your child's hands or other circumscribed, repeated movements, even those that are self-injurious or destructive to others or property.

In children with AS these perseverative behaviors may diminish and give way to obsessive interests, usually topical in nature, as the child gets older. This is exemplified by obsessive fascination with a particular narrow field such as sharks, weather, train schedules, airport architecture, maps, and so on. The pursuit of a very limited area of knowledge may encompass a huge amount of detail on the subject. Such persons seem to display an exquisite ability to memorize the smallest facts. In discussion on their favorite topic, they can, like Stanley in our opening example, "nitpick" over the smallest details. In our example in Chapter 1, Grandpa may think he remembers World War II, but his grandson with AS has memorized the details of the war with far greater accuracy. Clearly, the student can display perfectionism in building such a base of information. For this reason, AS has been compared in such respects to obsessive compulsive disorder. Autistic children who are later found not to be categorized as having AS may tend to display stereotypical behaviors longer and at levels that are difficult to extinguish. In many cases, physical perseverative behaviors decrease significantly over time in students with AS, and, in some cases, only obsessive thinking is perseverative in students with AS.

Use of Memory in Systemizing

Based on data from psychological testing, it is likely that the memory of the person with AS may not be better than others in general, but the huge collection of facts he or she knows probably represents the amount of time and effort that has gone into accumulating knowledge on one or two subjects to the exclusion of much else. The obsessions are not necessarily characterized by memorization of data alone. The term *systemizing* applies to the fascination with data that has inherent networks, such as maps, weather patterns, or airline schedules. Although it is commonly thought that obsessions can be strengths that can be utilized in the educational process, these obsessions can interfere significantly with other important daily functions (Russell & Sofronoff, 2005). Baron-Cohen, O'Riordan, Stone, Jones, and Plaisted (1999) postulate that children with AS are more interested in systems that can be described as "folk physics" (an interest in how things work) versus "folk psychology" (an interest in how people work). But, we have found that in female adolescents with AS, obsessions can include some human material, such as Hollywood celebrity facts. And, World War II and other military buffs with AS sometimes focus on the more human aspect of famous military decisions by war commanders. However, the knowledge collected by students with AS is generally focused on crystallized facts instead of interpersonal processes.

Language Development

Language seems to develop on time in children with AS, but words, while formulated according to the rules, seem to lack functional effectiveness, because they most often are used to express immediate needs or to expound on the child's favorite subjects. The child with AS seems not to see the main idea or the pivotal point. Children with AS tend to have problems with abstraction, inference, or practical, functional language. Their semantic understanding is limited, which frequently shows up in tests and instructional measures of listening comprehension. A major reason persons with AS are often referred to as "little professors" is due to their stiff and often pedantic and monotonic use of language. The varied, expressive qualities of expressive language may be unusual. This is called *prosody*, which is the pitch, loudness, tempo, stress emphasis, tonality, and rhythm patterns of spoken language.

Social Development

Beyond his interactions with parents, an AS child's slow social development extends to early play dates or simple play opportunities in which the child finds fascination with a toy and decides not to join in a sharing opportunity at another child's invitation. Kids with AS appear to lack the ability to articulate emotional attachment or to extend relationships to unfamiliar adults or peers. What psychologists call *parallel play* seems extended in the development of children with AS. In parallel play, children might enjoy toys near each other, but they don't interact in sharing toys or games with each other. The child with AS may play a game with others, but will not initiate the opportunity and may derive little pleasure from it. These children often require coaxing, prodding, or encouragement to maintain participation in games or group activities.

The child with AS may play a game with others, but will not initiate the opportunity and may derive little pleasure from it. These children often require coaxing, prodding, or encouragement to maintain participation in games or group activities.

There may be more than one process operating in social skills deficits. On one level, there is the ability to recognize emotions through reading faces, body posture, and voice inflection, and on another, the ability to make good judgments using the information obtained from "reading" others. Johnson (2004) suggests that social deficits may be due to a lack of integration among various perceptual and intellectual abilities, as well as social memory or recall.

One critical area of experience for persons with AS are social faux pas. Baron-Cohen and his colleagues (1999) have theorized about the mental functions that contribute to these mistakes. The term for the analysis of these embarrassing situations after the fact is *social autopsy*. This is a method that can be used in counseling or coaching children with AS, by helping them to dissect and correct what went wrong in a social interchange.

Behavior Problems

Although behavior problems are not unusual at home or school, they are not always a major presenting problem in AS. Negative behavioral outbursts are most frequently related to frustration, being thwarted, or difficulties in compliance when a particularly rigid response pattern has been challenged or interrupted. Oppositional behavior is sometimes found when areas of rigidity are challenged. Rebecca Moyes (2002), a parent of a child with AS, has presented a viewpoint on the development of behavior management plans for children with AS. She stresses the importance of first attempting to analyze the communicative intent of the negative behavior. A harsh, punitive approach to negative behavior is especially ill advised when the negative behavior was intended to communicate the child's feelings.

Theory of Mind

The solitary lack of engagement with others may develop to some degree into what can be described as a lifelong egocentrism or apparent selfishness. Your child may seem narcissistically concerned only with his or her own needs. What it reflects is a delay in the development of the idea that the self is equal in importance to that of others. This connects to an idea referred to in the research literature as *theory of mind*, or the ability to understand that others have minds, a point of view, feelings, and priorities. Theory of mind involves the ability to attribute mental states to others or to be able to describe what others might be feeling in a given situation.

Some researchers believe that the ability to guess others' states of mind is related to one's ability to effectively practice introspection on one's own. Some of these things can be acquired late in life and learned. The inability to guess others' mental states can result not only in faux pas but also in paranoia, by attributing negative intentions in others that aren't there. Blackshaw, Kinderman, Hare, and Hatton (2001) found that the lack of developed private self-consciousness was a predictor of paranoia. This suggests, again, that the ability to know one's self in some way may relate to our skill in attributing feelings and motivations to others. More severely autistic individuals may lack these facilities. Because of these deficits, persons with AS generally will take statements by others in a more concrete and literal fashion (Kaland et al., 2002). Williams (2004) suggests that, at the very least, people with AS must work harder at theorizing what others are experiencing than most persons. Educationally, this means that children with AS need more prompt questions and more time than others to understand social subtleties in language, such as irony, sarcasm, and some forms of humor.

Rigidity

One frequently observed feature of AS is rigidity in thought and behavior. Rigidity seems to pervade so many areas of the lives of people with AS. Novel situations often produce anxiety for these children. They may be uncomfortable with change in general. This can result in behavior that may be viewed as oppositional and can lead to emotional meltdowns. This general rigidity is what parents, neighbors, and teachers often label as stubbornness. Children with AS may have many fears in addition to those related to unexpected changes in schedules. Large groups of people and complex, open environments like school hallways, cafeterias, playgrounds, or bus stations tend to overwhelm kids with AS. They may also be overwhelmed by unexpected academic challenge or by having too many things to remember or too many tasks to perform. They often have limited frustration tolerance and may display tantrums when thwarted. Routines and rules are very important to children with AS in providing a sense of needed order and structure, and hence, predictability about the world. More will be discussed about the need to ease children into changes in school or class routines in Chapter 6.

Another form or rigidity is moralism, a kind of self-righteous and inflexible adherence to nonnegotiable moral principles that is often out of context with practical reality. An example might be a child who criticizes a parent who has run a yellow traffic light when the parent is on the way to the emergency room for treatment of a severe cut or burn. Rigidity is also found in the inflexibility over matters that are of little consequence, such as arguing about whether the route to the emergency room was the quickest when it might be the difference between a few hundred yards by choosing to take one turn over another. In the classroom, this may be found when a student fixates on a perception that a teacher has not enforced a rule consistently. Such fixations on moral correctness can escalate and interfere with availability for instruction.

School Concerns for Students With AS

Just as parents have difficulties in identifying the early signs of AS, teachers also may be uncertain of key features to address educationally. During the individual development of the child, parents and teachers must take notice as skills blossom or fail to develop as expected. Many children suspected of AS are brought to the psychiatry, psychology, or early childhood departments of pediatric medical centers. Other children with AS in the U.S. are spotted as having unique delays by child find screenings and soon receive pull-out or part-time programs for preschool children with developmental delays. They frequently require speech/language, occupational, and physical therapy interventions. They are monitored for further crystallization of symptoms. Frequently, behavior management programs and parent support programs are employed.

There are many jurisdictions, however, where these early assessment and intervention opportunities are not in place. Early on, children suspected of delays might be classified in general as having pervasive developmental disorders, an umbrella category for many of the varieties of autism. They may be seen as multiply handicapped or multiply disabled. They may be placed in a diagnostic center or in a diagnostic mode while they are being monitored. Schools are some of the best laboratories for differentiating appropriate classification schemes, as the strengths and weaknesses crystallize in the child's attempts to absorb, adapt to, and master the world of learning. The problems children with AS face in school will be covered in greater detail in Chapters 5 and 6. Tips for helping your child succeed in school are included in Chapters 7 and 8.

Schools are some of the best laboratories for differentiating appropriate classification schemes, as the strengths and weaknesses crystallize in the child's attempts to absorb, adapt to, and master the world of learning.

Community Concerns for Persons With AS

The primary aspect of AS that characterizes it as autistic is the problem of human connectedness. The term most commonly used to describe this core weakness of human connection is *reciprocity*. This refers to the individual's ability to engage other people in a way that makes others feel connected or not. In adult social conversation with a person with AS, eye contact is often poor, fleeting, or absent. The person with AS may not be able to read subtle gestures and facial changes or to interpret subtleties in language such as irony or sarcasm. They do not read or respond as most people do to small changes in body posture or to gestures. They seem either distant, stiff, or in other ways unconnected. Persons with AS not only seem disconnected, but in some cases uninterested in being in relationships with others. They may generally have very little interest in the feelings, experiences, other human qualities, or possibilities of others and, hence, lack empathy. They do not seem to derive pleasure from engaging others, learning about them, talking with them, or sharing experiences. In the many cases where the symptoms are milder, the individual may wish to connect with others but simply does not know how. They may have feelings for others but can't seem to mobilize the demonstration of those feelings.

At first, neurotypical ("normal") people in common social contexts (such as around the water cooler at work) may see people with AS as shy and retiring, quiet, stiff, or withdrawn. As the uninitiated begin to talk with persons with AS, it may appear that they seem to respond robotically. They have a monotonic voice that often comes across as reminiscent of the aforementioned geeks or nerds. The initial impression is that one is dealing with an eccentric. People with AS, including children, seem to lack warmth to their more socially apt peers. There is a sense that the person with AS just isn't there when he or she is interacting with you. He may not know what to do when someone has finished making a point. She may not know when to stop talking and may seem overly interested in her topic of conversation and not yours, unless you are equally fascinated with her areas of interest. All too frequently, however, persons with AS seem not just alien and unconnected, but preoccupied with one or two subjects, which they will talk about endlessly. They may take offense easily over unrelated trifles or become upset when others do not share their enthusiasm for a given area of interest. There is a kind of immaturity or somewhat fixed developmental delay, in which the needs, interests, feelings, perspectives, and thoughts of others just aren't real or important to them. Intervention in teaching about the lives of others is important here.

In conversation with a person with AS, you may find yourself doing most of the work in the exchange, asking most of the questions, and waiting for obvious follow-ups that don't occur. His frequently robotic language and responses seem to suggest that others might as well be inanimate. It is not just a question of only lacking the ability to read social cues. There is an output problem, not knowing how to engage and maintain relationships with others, and most certainly an internal problem, in which social/emotional information is absent, confusing, undeveloped, and/or not valued. He may not have labels for feelings. The person with AS may seem odd, making you uncomfortable. The simplest conversation among neurotypical people is kind of a naturalistic dance, a flowing interchange of cues and fitting responses. Because there really is quite a lack of tolerance in the workplace for not being able to engage in this kind of behavior (especially with the workplace being the "gossip mill" that it normally is), a person with AS soon becomes grist for that gossip mill and finds himself unemployed for vague reasons. It is difficult not to overemphasize the power of having the appearance of being a "regular person" in the workplace.

"Aspies," as adult persons with AS sometimes like to refer to themselves when they congregate physically or in Internet chat rooms, are often quite aware as they get older that there are differences between themselves and normal or neurotypical persons who they call "NT's." They may spend a lifetime trying to identify and adjust to those differences if they do not shut down their attempts to try. Aspies have created their own "in groups," support groups, and Web sites where they feel valued and where their strengths are valued. Writers like Temple Grandin have spent many years explaining to the rest of us these experiences in learning, adjusting, and living shared by persons with AS. There is an excellent portrayal of a young adult with AS by Josh Hartnett in the film *Mozart and the Whale*. In his portrayal, Hartnett appears to convincingly embody all of the characteristics and many of the challenges of a person with AS. The lead character demonstrates considerable awareness of the challenges associated with AS and shows adaptation to the world of people with neurodevelopmental differences and the world at large.

When parents recognize these characteristics, it is helpful to make note of them when meeting professionals for the first time. In the following chapter, we will discuss how professionals will utilize the parents' observations and discoveries in making diagnoses and recommending interventions.

chapter 3

Recognizing and Diagnosing AS

CONCERNED about her lack of progress both at home and in preschool, Celia's parents finally came to agreement that they needed to find out what might be the cause of her problems. A close friend recommended a pediatrician, who focused on her inattentiveness and diagnosed attention deficit/hyperactivity disorder (ADHD). Celia's mother had a gut feeling that there must be something more. ADHD didn't explain Celia's lack of social connection, her perseverative focus on certain topics, or her difficult behavior when asked to transition to new activities or participate in a group. Celia's teacher suggested that the parents have her evaluated by a behavioral specialist, who diagnosed oppositional defiant disorder, which again didn't seem to completely explain the causes or solutions to Celia's unique set of challenges. As she entered kindergarten and then first grade, the discrepancy between how obviously bright she was and how strong her reading was, with her poor performance in writing and math led Celia's parents to request a psychoeducational evaluation, which suggested probable learning disabilities. It was not until third grade that a knowledgeable teacher and school psychologist took a fresh look at Celia's case. Subsequently, AS was accurately diagnosed as the source of Celia's struggles. This opened the door to a better understanding of Celia's strengths and needs and led to getting appropriate services in the school and in the community.

The diagnosis of AS is considerably challenging for many professionals. It certainly can be difficult for parents who are concerned about their children. Many parents naturally turn to the Internet or friends to find available guidelines for diagnostic classifications. Parents' observations and intimate knowledge of their

Myths in the Diagnosis of AS

The following are unproven myths about the identification of AS:

- All persons with AS can be identified by their stronger verbal than performance IQs.
- All persons with AS have above-average intelligence.
- People with AS all want to communicate with others but don't know how.
- People with AS don't want to communicate with others.
- All "nerdy" people have a touch of AS.
- AS and high-functioning autism (HFA) are the same.
- Autism is a perfect spectrum or continuity of symptom intensity and frequency.
- A high number of autistic symptoms rules out functional capacity in persons with AS or other forms of autism.
- Persons with AS have higher adaptive abilities than persons with high-functioning autism.

child's development are important sources in working with professionals to arrive at an accurate diagnosis. In this chapter, we hope to explain how professionals, parents, and other stakeholders are becoming more precise in determining diagnosis. Parents, we do emphasize that only a trained mental health professional is qualified to make an accurate diagnosis. Please do not attempt to diagnose your child on your own or trust in the accuracy and reliability of Internet-based tests and checklists.

The Genetic Possibilities

As research on early child development and early parent/child interaction expands, we not only will know more about identifying autism in general but also will be able to identify more specific forms earlier through observable behaviors, especially as specific markers in development occur. Eventually, there may be a genetic test for the disorder such as the one used to detect Down's syndrome. Gillberg and Cederlund (2005) commented that about 50% of boys with AS have a paternal history of autism spectrum disorder. Pre- and perinatal risks appeared to be important in about 25% of cases. These could involve such factors as prenatal exposure to alcohol, oxygen insufficiency at birth, or postnatal hyperbilirubinemia. Neonatal hyperbilirubinemia, or jaundice, medically defined as a total serum bilirubin level above 5 milligrams per deciliter, is a frequently encountered problem in up to 60% of full-term newborns. Abnormal metabolites produced in genetic disorders like phenylketonuria (PKU) may impede brain development in similar ways. PKU is an inherited error of metabolism caused by a deficiency in the enzyme phenylalanine hydroxylase. Loss of this enzyme results in mental retardation, organ damage, and unusual posture and can, in cases of maternal PKU, severely compromise pregnancy.

Klin et al. (2000) reviewed the available data on family genetic studies in AS and related conditions. Although the data was scant, they suggested that AS, autism, and a broader autism phenotype may be genetically related to one another. Some studies have found schizophrenia in the family histories of persons with AS. This raises the question, though, whether some adults diagnosed with schizophrenia in later life may, in fact, have had AS. The first genome-wide screen for AS was reported in *Molecular Psychiatry* by Ylisaukko-oja and colleagues (2004). In this screening, the researchers found an overlap between a suspected autism susceptibility locus and a reported schizophrenia susceptibility locus. Recently, a group led by Durand (2006) reported on a mutation of a single part of chromosome 22q13, which can result in language and/or social communication disorders. These mutations concern only a small number of individuals, but they shed light on one gene dosage-sensitive synaptic pathway that may be involved in autism spectrum disorders. As the research in this area becomes more refined, it is likely that the genetic profile of AS will be discovered.

Early Identification

Charman, Howlin, Berry, and Prince (2004) conducted a study that included the diagnostic experiences of parents of children with autism and parents of children identified with AS in Great Britain. Results demonstrated that parents of children diagnosed as autistic typically became aware of problems in the child's development at an earlier age than parents of children with AS. They sought help earlier and received a diagnosis much sooner. The average age of the child when he or she was diagnosed with AS was 11.13 years compared to 5.49 years for autism. Generally, a clear diagnosis of AS is not made for most children until they are of school age (McConachie, Le Couteur, & Honey, 2005).

Critical research is now ongoing in efforts to make the accurate diagnosis of AS as early as possible. It has been clearly demonstrated with other forms of autism that early, intensive intervention makes a great difference in the future of the child with autism. It is extremely important, then, that AS be identified early in order to protect and enrich the quality of life of these children.

Why Is Accurate Diagnosis Important?

What we know of adults living with the disorder without benefit of accurate diagnosis early in life is that they suffer in independent living, their social life, and the world of work. Frequently, significant emotional problems and even mental illness may result from this developmental disability. Fortunately, diagnosis and intervention at any age can be helpful.

AS is not so much something that someone "has" or a disease that one has contracted, as it is a whole personality that is atypical. It is something someone "is." Although AS falls on the autism spectrum, which encompasses a range of disorders with some core similarities, it is very much by itself in its consistency of symptoms and personal strengths and weaknesses, despite debates in the professional research literature. Asperger's syndrome is a unique way of seeing, interpreting, coping with, and acting in the world.

Asperger's syndrome is a unique way of seeing, interpreting, coping with, and acting in the world.

Because AS is quite hard-wired, the diagnosis helps to direct parents and teachers to lifelong interventions appropriate to the condition. Failure to identify it, and to do so early, may doom parents and teachers to set goals and expectations that are unrealistic and disappointing. In the past, many mental health professionals misdiagnosed the patient as having something else or didn't know what they were dealing with. Many adults with AS were thought to be paranoid, because they sometimes became increasingly defensive as their attempts to relate to others failed through misinterpretation of others' behaviors and motives. They lost trust in others as they lost trust in themselves and in their ability to effectively interpret, and hence, manipulate the social environment.

Making the Diagnosis

Mental health professionals such as psychiatrists, clinical psychologists, school psychologists, licensed professional counselors, and social workers often are the first to make the diagnosis of Asperger's syndrome and they need clear guidelines to help them make this identification. Again, parents and teachers should not attempt to make this diagnosis on their own. Seek out diagnoses from a qualified and experienced mental health professional working in this field.

Although there are many seasoned clinicians who can quickly make a clear identification of AS, there is a variability of standards for defining what it is and what it isn't. Gillberg, Gillberg, Rastam, and Wentz (2001) point out that there were no published rating scales prior to 2001. Therefore, the development of scales to determine AS has been hampered by a lack of agreement about what to include and not include in the definition. Howlin (2000) reviewed assessment instruments for AS, noting that differences in classification systems limited the development of accurate measures. There are currently about five rating scales in use or under development for identifying AS and differentiating it from other conditions. Thus far, few of these instruments have had adequate sample sizes or rigorous statistical analyses. Recently, Jonathan M. Campbell (2005) reviewed and compared the strengths and weaknesses of the five rating scales for AS: the Asperger Syndrome Diagnostic

Scale (ASDS), the Autism Spectrum Screening Questionnaire (ASSQ), the Childhood Asperger Syndrome Test (CAST), Gilliam Asperger's Disorder Scale (GADS), and Krug Asperger's Disorder Index (KADI). The KADI appeared to be the most thorough in terms of item selection. The ASSQ appeared to be the most reliable test, but has less convincing validity. In other words, test scores appear to be consistent over time, but may not be helpful in predicting actual diagnoses. The CAST displayed good predictive validity in the absence of published reliability studies (Campbell, 2005). All published rating scales demonstrate significant weaknesses, particularly those with questionable normative samples. Research on these measures is being continued and refined. Parents and adults with AS are cautioned about taking rating scale tests on the Internet until appropriately standardized and statistically validated measures with meaningful cut-off scores are developed. At the present time, many rating scales lack the sensitivity required for accurate diagnosis alone. Therefore, classification into diagnostic categories should not be made on the basis of one instrument alone.

The *DSM-IV*, the fourth edition of the *Diagnostic and Statistical Manual* of the American Psychiatric Association, is the handbook for those in the mental health professions qualified to make diagnoses. AS, along with all of the forms of autism, is identified under the general classification of pervasive developmental disorders (PDDs). Let's take a look at the DSM-IV diagnostic criteria. AS is diagnosed by the presence of the following behavioral characteristics.

I) Qualitative impairment in social interaction, as manifested by at least two of the following:

(A) marked impairments in the use of multiple nonverbal behaviors such as eye-to-eye gaze, facial expression, body posture, and gestures to regulate social interaction

(B) failure to develop peer relationships appropriate to developmental level

(C) a lack of spontaneous seeking to share enjoyment, interest or achievements with other people, (e.g., by a lack of showing, bringing, or pointing out objects of interest to other people)

(D) lack of social or emotional reciprocity

(II) Restricted repetitive and stereotyped patterns of behavior, interests and activities, as manifested by at least one of the following:

(A) encompassing preoccupation with one or more stereotyped and restricted patterns of interest that is abnormal either in intensity or focus

(B) apparently inflexible adherence to specific, non-functional routines or rituals

(C) stereotyped and repetitive motor mannerisms (e.g. hand or finger flapping or twisting, or complex whole-body movements)

(D) persistent preoccupation with parts of objects

(III) The disturbance causes clinically significant impairments in social, occupational, or other important areas of functioning.

(IV) There is no clinically significant general delay in language (e.g., single words used by age 2 years, communicative phrases used by age 3 years).

(V) There is no clinically significant delay in cognitive development or in the development of age-appropriate self help skills, adaptive behavior (other than in social interaction) and curiosity about the environment in childhood.

(VI) Criteria are not met for another specific Pervasive Developmental Disorder or Schizophrenia. (American Psychiatric Association, 1994, p. 77)

These are the some of the same criteria needed for a diagnosis of autism, with one major exception. The criteria for diagnosing autism include the presence of severe language delays. With AS, these delays are usually not present; however, clinical experience and research reveal that there are differences in the use of language by persons with AS.

Although many of the features of advanced language are present in children with AS in terms of the sophistication of formulating and making connections within language networks, there is a critical lack of ability to employ language interactively to practical ends, except to make requests or demands or to inform others of details that might not be relevant to anyone else's interests. There are differences in pace and prosody (the rhythm of words and stressing of syllables). Ghaziuddin and Gerstein's research (1996) suggests that the pedantic speech of people with AS is helpful in differentiating the diagnosis of AS from high-functioning autism. However, persons with AS' ability to exhibit well-formed, complex speech patterns is superior to other forms of autism, including high-functioning autism.

The *DSM-IV* notes that there are no significant cognitive delays in children with AS. However, research suggests that there may be interesting intellectual strengths and weaknesses frequently found in children with AS. Most experienced clinicians have identified stronger verbal than performance or visual/spatial intelligence test scores. This is not true in every case, as there are talented artists who have strong visual/spatial skills with AS. Generally, the data support the idea of a strong verbal ability being present in kids with Asperger's. A study by Ghaziuddin and Mountain-Kimchi (2004) confirmed this view. Parents and educators are urged to be cautious when looking at IQ test profiles. The interpretation of IQ test profiles is best left to persons with an advanced understanding of testing, such as clinical and school psychologists. There are many reasons why IQ subtest comparisons are dangerous. For one thing, the difference between two tested skills on the surface may seem to be very meaningful, but may, in fact, not be statistically significant. Often, far too much is made of differences between types of items in IQ tests, when those differences only display normal variation (Sattler, 2001). Also, there will always be some variation between skills on IQ tests over time in any individual. A skill may seem higher on one testing than another. Most IQ tests have technical tables used by professionals that help them determine when a difference between one skill and another is really statistically significant.

There are some patterns among the IQ scores of persons with AS that seem to emerge in clinical practice. People with AS can reason, but they don't seem to comprehend the core, vital, or central meaning being expressed when listening to or watching someone or something. They don't always seem to identify or register what is important. And, they may often lack the judgment to use information in making practical, wise decisions. On tests that require identification of key or missing elements, they often miss obvious details, because they do not know what to scan for. Or, they may focus on a detail that is irrelevant that no one has thought of before. Myles and Simpson (1998) point out that students with AS frequently lack common sense and an awareness of how to apply rules of social interchange flexibly to adapt to various contexts. Their level of vocabulary and amount of pure verbosity may lead the listener to assume that they have good inferential skills, when, in fact, they are unable to make appropriate abstractions from the facts that they collect. Mottron (2004) reported that the ability to label things verbally was one of the strongest verbal skills in high-functioning persons with PDDs. However, students with AS may demonstrate good vocabulary skills on tests and in the classroom, but their practical comprehension may not be at the same level. Persons

People with AS can reason, but they don't seem to comprehend the core, vital, or central meaning being expressed when listening to or watching someone or something.

with AS are often quite unaware of their comprehension deficits or may be very guarded about having them pointed out by others, easily taking offense. For them, the world may seem increasingly complicated, overwhelming, and even dangerous because of these practical comprehension problems.

The intellectual habits of persons with AS, while perhaps apparently systemized, are not usually very efficient. So, their thinking patterns may be incomplete, inadequate, or often not very adaptive to situations or changes in situations. On the other hand, because persons with AS may not see things from the expected angle that most other people do, they may come up with very surprising, clever, unique interpretations, associations, or solutions for problems that no one else has thought of before. If a person with AS has a sense of humor, he may find things funny that others don't "get" or he may come up with hilarious associations that most people wouldn't think of.

Differential Diagnosis

The process of identifying a person as belonging to one diagnostic category as opposed to another with similar characteristics is called *differential diagnosis.* There are a number of conditions that overlap with AS. Some of them are social skills deficits, social anxiety, hyperlexia, nonverbal learning disabilities, high-functioning autism, pervasive developmental disorder–not otherwise specified, and semantic/pragmatic disorder.

We have mentioned previously that it is convenient to talk about related problems as lying along a continuum of severity. AS is also thought to be part of the high end of the autistic spectrum. This simplistic way of thinking of these issues has been challenged in convincing research by Szatmari (2000). He notes that since the *DSM-III*, clinicians have thought about disorders as discrete biological entities. At the same time, clinicians talk about them along continua. The *DSM-IV* is more helpful because diagnoses are formed on the basis of symptom patterns. Szatmari (2000) finds it more helpful to think about autistic and related disorders in terms of the following variables:

- functional ability (such as that found through measures of adaptive skills),
- symptom severity, and
- rate and quality of language development.

High-functioning autism (HFA) has also become confusing. Often it is interpreted as reflecting a higher IQ, while others use the term to refer to persons who have better adaptive skills, less symptomatic severity, and better language skills. There does not appear to be a conventional definition of HFA that delineates which of the above factors is being employed when the term is used. McLaughlin-Cheng (1998) found that children and adolescents with AS perform better than those with more classic autism on intelligence and cognitive measures, as well as measures of everyday adaptive behavior functioning. She felt her data supported the notion that AS and more classic autism can be seen as separate disorders. In the early 1990s, researchers simply thought AS was a mild form of HFA (Szatmari, Brenner, & Nagy, 1989). Recently, a study by Klin et al. (in press) found that Vineland Adaptive Behavior Scale scores of persons with AS and HFA were equally impaired. In a review of the literature, Kasari and Rotheram-Fuller (2005) noted that many studies continue to lump AS and HFA without distinguishing the two within research subject populations.

Persons with social skills deficits may be on a mild end of the autism spectrum. They may be functional in everyday life and lack all of the other characteristics of persons with AS. Social anxiety is a specific anxiety, as opposed to a full-time anxious state, that relates primarily to the apprehension about initiating social relationships or contact. Russell and Sofronoff (2005) demonstrated that children with AS have more obsessive-compulsive and physical injury worries than clinically anxious children. Although children with AS reveal more anxiety symptoms than the normal population, their profile is different from clinically anxious children.

Hyperlexia is a condition that some persons with AS have. It is a language disorder characterized by early precocious reading and/or intense fascination with letters and numbers. This is accompanied by limited comprehension of what is read, difficulty with verbal language, difficulties with social interaction, and other autistic traits. Many persons thought to have hyperlexia actually may have AS.

The more complex challenge for the teacher or parent is discriminating AS from nonverbal learning disabilities, high-functioning autism, and PDD-NOS. In 2005, Klin, Pauls, Schultz, and Volkmar proposed a new system of diagnosing AS. Their study demonstrated low agreement among three commonly used approaches and lead to different results in comparison of IQ profiles, patterns of coexisting conditions, and familial psychiatric patterns among high-functioning autism, AS, and PDD-NOS groups. Klin et al. (2005) proposed a new system that takes into account that: (a) children with AS isolate themselves less in early development (but are still inappropriate in their demand for attention), compared to classically autistic children; (b) children with AS have adequate or even precocious language, while the language of classically autistic children is delayed, echolalic, or otherwise stereotyped; (c) the presence of one-sided verbosity in children with AS as a necessary criterion; and (d) the presence of factual, circumscribed interests that interfere with both general learning and with reciprocal social conversation. The syndrome could be distinguished from general autism by IQ profiles where verbal comprehension is higher than perceptual reasoning skills. AS was distinguished from PDD-NOS based on the fact that it has fewer coexisting symptoms. Also, PDD-NOS was found by Walker et al. (2004) to have fewer autistic symptoms, especially stereotypic repetitive behaviors, than both autism and AS groups. Finally, AS is distinguished from PDD-NOS in that there is a higher genetic contribution to the former.

Ozonoff, South, and Miller (2000) studied 23 subjects with autism and 12 with AS. The subjects ranged in age from 6 to 20 and were carefully matched on a number of variables. Overall, it was found that the AS group demonstrated less severe early symptoms, a less problematic developmental course, and better outcome than the high-functioning autism group. To a large extent, differences in variables were matters of degree. Klin et al. (2005) also have agreed that the differential diagnosis is difficult in terms of adequate current research support, although there are observed clinical differences. The new system developed by Klin et al. (2005) provides more clarity by demonstrating statistically significant, pivotal markers that differentiate AS from other related conditions.

Rourke (1989) has demonstrated that a profile of intellectual and social deficits called nonverbal learning disabilities (NVLD) may mirror Asperger's. NVLD was first conceptualized by Johnson and Mykelbust (1967). NVLD includes deficits in tactile perception, psychomotor coordination, visual-spatial organization, nonverbal problem solving, lack of appreciation of incongruities and humor, difficulty in adapting to novel and complex situations, overreliance on rote behaviors, and relative deficits in mechanical arithmetic. Despite proficiencies in single-word reading, children with NVLD display poor pragmatics and prosody in speech and significant deficits in social perception, social judgment, and social interaction skills. Volkmar and Klin (1998) have pointed to overlaps in the concepts of AS and NVLD. Rourke and Tsatsanis (2000) also suggest that there may be points of correspondence between the clinical presentations of the two disorders. The difference is the degree of social impairment. Gunter, Ghaziuddin, and Ellis (2002) demonstrated a close similarity in the neuropsychological profiles of NVLD and AS.

From reading the above descriptions, it is evident that distinguishing AS from many similar conditions is a challenge not only for parents but also for clinicians. The aim of the assessment should be a detailed profile of the individual's strengths and needs, rather than simply a diagnostic label. We believe that effective educational and treatment programs can only be devised on the basis of such a profile, which provides a comprehensive portrait of the individual for purposeful and effective interventions.

Neurological "Soft Signs"

The following are features shared by a number of (but not all) neurological atypicalities and disorders and are often found in the autistic spectrum disorders. They do not necessarily act as pivotal features in making diagnoses, but they are important in recognizing that characteristics overlap between disorders. Because they offer important hints, these features are called *soft signs*, and must be addressed educationally. Often, these features are not addressed and prove to be frustrating to teachers. Parents are already familiar with these features from child rearing, but they don't always appear in specialist reports, because testing is often done in one-on-one conditions. They also often are not addressed in Individual Educational Plans (IEPs) or other school intervention plans, such as Section 504 plans. However, when they are addressed in IEPs and 504 plans they can make a world of difference in the way achievement targets can be met. These features include:

- irritability;
- motor automatisms like tics and tremors, including Tourette's syndrome;

- low frustration tolerance;
- fatigue;
- lack of perseverance;
- lack of resilience;
- rigidity and difficulties with transitions and change;
- stubbornness;
- oppositionality;
- perseveration—repeating actions, thoughts, verbalizations;
- emotional immaturity;
- emotional vulnerability;
- emotional lability (unpredictable propensity to change);
- impulsivity;
- explosiveness;
- auditory or visual perceptual discrimination errors;
- lack of thorough perceptual scanning;
- speech/language symptoms, especially articulation and slow and uneven pacing of words, and retrieval, hesitation, or immaturity in formulation;
- somatic complaints including headaches;
- gross and fine-motor awkwardness, poor coordination, or balance;
- sequential, short-term, and working memory problems;
- impaired social perception;
- impaired comprehension;
- limitations in judgment; and
- general problems in executive functioning.

The above characteristic in themselves are not diagnostic of any single disability and may not always be always present in AS or any of its possible coexisting conditions, however, they can be flags or markers to alert us to some of the barriers to classroom instruction.

Additional Characteristics

Little research has been conducted on existing normed personality tests for the use of identification of AS in adults. Because AS involves some commonly shared personality characteristics, there is hope that in the future there will be better accuracy in diagnosing AS when suspected in adulthood. Some of the work of Ozonoff, Garcia, Clark, and Lainhart (2005) is promising in using such instruments as the Minnesota Multiphasic Personality Inventory–2 (MMPI-2), which reveals some consistency in response patterns with adults.

The following are some characteristics from a list prepared by Roger N. Meyer, an adult who reported about his own AS experiences, and Tony Attwood (2001). Meyer notes that these characteristics are distinguished in adults with AS because of their consistency of appearance, intensity, and the high number of them that appear simultaneously. However, he also writes that not every one of these characteristics will apply to adults with AS.

Social Characteristics

- Difficulty in accepting criticism or correction.
- Difficulty in offering correction or criticism without appearing harsh, pedantic or insensitive.
- Difficulty in perceiving and applying unwritten social rules or protocols.
- "Immature" manners.

- Failure to distinguish between private and public personal care habits (i.e., brushing, public attention to skin problems, nose picking, teeth picking, ear canal cleaning, clothing arrangement).
- Naive trust in others.
- Shyness.
- Low or no conversational participation in group meetings or conferences.
- Constant anxiety about performance and acceptance, despite recognition and commendation.
- Scrupulous honesty, often expressed in an apparently disarming or inappropriate manner or setting.
- Bluntness in emotional expression.
- "Flat affect."
- Discomfort manipulating or "playing games" with others.
- Unmodulated reaction in being manipulated, patronized, or "handled" by others.
- Low to medium level of paranoia.
- Low to no apparent sense of humor; bizarre sense of humor (often stemming from a "private" internal thread of humor being inserted in public conversation without preparation or warming others up to the reason for the "punch line").
- Difficulty with reciprocal displays of pleasantries and greetings.
- Problems expressing empathy or comfort to/with others: sadness, condolence, congratulations, etc.
- Pouting, ruminating, fixating on bad experiences with people or events for an inordinate length of time.
- Difficulty with adopting a social mask to obscure real feelings, moods, reactions.

- Using social masks inappropriately.
- Abrupt and strong expression of likes and dislikes.
- Rigid adherence to rules and social conventions where flexibility is desirable.
- Apparent absence of relaxation, recreational, or "time out" activities.
- "Serious" all the time.
- Known for single-mindedness.
- Flash temper.
- Tantrums.
- Excessive talk.
- Difficulty in forming friendships and intimate relationships; difficulty in distinguishing between acquaintance and friendship.
- Social isolation and intense concern for privacy.
- Limited clothing preference; discomfort with formal attire or uniforms.
- Preference for bland or bare environments in living arrangements.
- Difficulty judging others' personal space.
- Limited by intensely pursued interests.
- Often perceived as "being in their own world."

Physical Manifestations

- Strong sensory sensitivities: touch and tactile sensations, sounds, lighting and colors, odors, taste.
- Clumsiness.
- Balance difficulties.

- Difficulty in judging distances, height, depth.
- Difficulty in recognizing others' faces (prosopagnosia).
- Stims (self-stimulatory behavior serving to reduce anxiety, stress, or to express pleasure).
- Self-injurious or disfiguring behaviors.
- Nail-biting.
- Unusual gait, stance, posture.
- Gross or fine motor coordination problems.
- Low apparent sexual interest.
- Depression.
- Anxiety.
- Sleep difficulties.
- Verbosity.
- Difficulty expressing anger (excessive or "bottled up").
- Flat or monotone vocal expression; limited range of inflection.
- Difficulty with initiating or maintaining eye contact.
- Elevated voice volume during periods of stress and frustration.
- Strong food preferences and aversions.
- Unusual and rigidly adhered to eating behaviors.
- Bad or unusual personal hygiene.

Cognitive Characteristics

- Susceptibility to distraction.
- Difficulty in expressing emotions.
- Resistance to or failure to respond to talk therapy.
- Mental shutdown response to conflicting demands and multi-tasking.

- Generalized confusion during periods of stress.
- Low understanding of the reciprocal rules of conversation: interrupting, dominating, minimum participation, difficult in shifting topics, problem with initiating or terminating conversation, subject perseveration.
- Insensitivity to the non-verbal cues of others (stance, posture, facial expressions).
- Perseveration best characterized by the term "bulldog tenacity."
- Literal interpretation of instructions (failure to read between the lines).
- Interpreting words and phrases literally (problem with colloquialisms, clichés, neologism, turns of phrase, common humorous expressions).
- Preference for visually oriented instruction and training.
- Dependence on step-by-step learning procedures (disorientation occurs when a step is assumed, deleted, or otherwise overlooked in instruction).
- Difficulty in generalizing.
- Preference for repetitive, often simple routines.
- Difficulty in understanding rules for games of social entertainment.
- Missing or misconstruing others' agendas, priorities, preferences.
- Impulsiveness.
- Compelling need to finish one task completely before starting another.
- Rigid adherence to rules and routines.
- Difficulty in interpreting meaning to others' activities; difficulty in drawing relationships between an activity or event and ideas.

- Exquisite attention to detail, principally visual, or details that can be visualized ("Thinking in Pictures") or cognitive details (often those learned by rote).
- Concrete thinking.
- Distractibility due to focus on external or internal sensations, thoughts, and/or sensory input (appearing to be in a world of one's own or day-dreaming).
- Difficulty in assessing relative importance of details (an aspect of the trees/forest problem).
- Poor judgment of when a task is finished (often attributable to perfectionism or an apparent unwillingness to follow differential standards for quality).
- Difficulty in imagining others' thoughts in a similar or identical event or circumstance that are different from one's own ("Theory of Mind" issues).
- Difficulty with organizing and sequencing (planning and execution; successful performance of tasks in a logical, functional order).
- Difficulty in assessing cause and effect relationships (behaviors and consequences).
- An apparent lack of "common sense."
- Relaxation techniques and developing recreational "release" interest may require formal instruction.
- Rage, tantrum, shutdown, self-isolating reactions appearing "out of nowhere."
- Substantial hidden self-anger, anger towards others, and resentment.
- Difficulty in estimating time to complete tasks.
- Difficulty in learning self-monitoring techniques.
- Disinclination to produce expected results in an orthodox manner.

- Psychometric testing shows great deviance between verbal and performance results.
- Extreme reaction to changes in routine, surroundings, and people.
- Stilted, pedantic conversational style ("The Professor").

Note. From *Asperger Syndrome Employment Workbook: An Employment Workbook for Adults With Asperger Syndrome* (p. 306), by R. N. Meyer and T. Attwood, 2001, Philadelphia: Jessica Kingsley. Copyright © 2001 Jessica Kingsley. Reprinted by permission of Jessica Kingsley Publishers..

The Neurology and Neuropsychology of AS

Researchers are only just beginning the quest to discover which neurological structures are involved in AS. At the present time it is not clear as to what specific parts of the brain are related to AS. Different studies around the world have obtained different findings. Some studies have found enlargement of the folds or convolutions of the brain in some areas where there appears to be neuronal migration programmed from early in life. Other studies reveal many smaller folds that seem different from the brains of neurotypical persons. Brain imaging techniques like positron emission tomography (PET) and single photon emission computed tomography (SPECT) are very promising because they can actually illuminate and show pictures of parts of the brain in action while subjects are performing tasks. For example, when Schultz et al. (2000) showed pictures of faces to autistic patients, they found little activation in a face processing area called FFA, but did find a high level of activity in a nearby brain region associated with recognizing objects. In this case, the researchers used MRI technology to discover this brain activity. Critchley et al. (2000) also found a failure to activate regions with electrical activity in the face processing area when appraising emotional facial expressions.

When looking for relationships between moving geometric shapes and brain areas, Schultz and colleagues (2000) found that social-like cooperative movements between the shapes correlated with the FFA, leading them to determine that the FFA may not only deal with recognizing faces, but also with recognizing perceptions and interactions that are social in nature. They refer to the "social brain" as the interconnected network of regions that includes the amygdala, the medial frontal cortex, the superior temporal sulcus, and the FFA (Schultz et al., 2000).

Similar functional studies of the brain in action can be reflected through SPECT scans, which determine blood flow differences using different colors. These techniques may lead to identification of reliable areas of the brains of persons with AS that differ from neurotypical subjects. The first SPECT study in a patient with AS that was published found parietooccipital hypoperfusion or decreased blood flow in the top rear section of the brain. The important concept to keep in mind about the neurology of AS is that, in the vast majority of cases, the differences in the brain are not caused by lesions or insult to the brain, but are differences in the development of brain areas either by size, migration of cells during development, or a lack of richness of connectivity and networking within structures. These atypicalities in brain development appear to be part of the unfolding of the unique genetic programming of individuals with AS.

Precautions in the Assessment of Autism and AS

The assessment of children with autistic spectrum disorders may be compromised by several factors. Rating scales administered to significant stakeholders in the child's life have proven to be valid and reliable, but they are subject to bias. Defensiveness, optimism, and other general impressions and expectations can color the accuracy of ratings. Hence, multiple raters should be employed. Furthermore, it is very important that ratings are administered across two or more settings, especially in the case of adaptive measures. Children with AS may display significant immaturity in the development of independent, adaptive, self-care skills. This is not to be confused with the absence of skills found in mental retardation.

Although assessment of children with AS or any other form of autism is crucial, it may also be very problematic. Professionals with specific experience in dealing with this population should conduct assessments of children suspected of having AS. Scores, particularly IQ scores, must be viewed with caution. The following are among considerations to take when administering direct assessment techniques to the child:

- Students with autistic spectrum disorders experience irregular, incomplete, and delayed emergence of developmental systems. Many normed test instruments may assume a fixed, incremental developmental sequence, which is not present in students with AS.
- Autism, by definition, is almost always accompanied by deficits in the ability to have typical bonding experiences with others. Reciprocal social contact is generally a significant weakness. To be accurate, most tests require a working level of rapport that cannot always be assumed to exist in children with autism. Adapted interpersonal cueing methods are often needed, and frequently improvised, to be clear that the child registers stimulus and response demands.
- Children with autism often have receptive and expressive language problems related to general communication deficits. Test selection must be carefully attempted to circumvent or avoid these issues, because test items requiring a high level of communication will not yield valid results. Simplified instructions are usually necessary. Items that

require formulated, lengthy verbal responses frequently are not appropriate.

- Children with autism often display attention deficits, either in more classic forms such as in ADHD or more frequently as a coexisting aspect of the condition. In general, this may limit the length of the strings of instructional wording that can be held in their working memories. They may not recognize the relevance and importance of stimuli that normally are targeted by typical children. Children with autism cannot be assumed to be able to identify the salient characteristics of stimuli presented to them without specific directions to do so.
- Sustained effort in attending, participating, and completing assessments or assessment items may require the presence of other adults familiar to the child, such as the child's teacher or paraeducator aide in cases when the child's symptoms would otherwise block access to instructions and participation in general. Many tests and best practices assume that there are no helpers, including parents, involved in the one-on-one testing process.
- Sustained effort in attending, participating, and completing assessments or assessment items may require the use of systems of behavioral modification, rewards, and other reinforcements. Children with autism may require very personally engineered external incentive systems for completing tasks that most children might not require.
- Children with autism have difficulty making transitions from one activity to another and with comprehending and registering new rules for unfamiliar tasks. Changing from one test item's demand to another may not be smooth. It cannot be assumed that children with autistic spectrum symptoms are able to generalize and sustain the instructional set or demands from one subtest item to the next.

- Children with autism often lack frustration tolerance for extended mental effort as required by many test instruments. Testing may require more frequent breaks and more test sessions.
- Children with autism or AS may not understand timed tasks and the need to hurry or be efficient. The fact that a test is timed is not always fully grasped by many students with neurological disorders. It should be determined that the student being tested fully understands the test item task requirement, or the item should not be administered. Because of the standardized nature of these tests, the instructions or expectations cannot be modified. Significant modifications to any instruction or item reduce the accuracy of the measures obtained.
- Pattern analysis of IQ tests of persons with AS suggests that there may also be problems with visual-motor speed, especially when using a writing implement (such as a pen or pencil). In addition, children with AS may have slow processing speed. All too often, processing speed is only measured on tests that require a pencil. Processing speed is a simple term that can include many parts in a mental activity and is almost never specified. For example, it may include retrieval of facts or action routines. It may include the actual internal, sequential execution of a series of steps. It may include the initiation or beginning of a task and formulation of a new strategy or other utilization of memory. Tests of visual-motor speed, especially with a pencil, are often included in IQ tests. Because motor awkwardness is a characteristic of AS, these subtests tend to pull IQ test scores artificially downward. Many test developers have argued against having motor-speeded tests included as part of the IQ examination, but most popular tests still employ them. So, when the term *processing speed* is referred to in a test as an index of ability,

it almost always refers to a complex assortment of actions in one task that usually has a motor requirement.

Many school systems use purely visual tests like the Raven's Progressive Matrices to determine giftedness. Some kids with AS also are gifted, but often are not identified as such. This primarily visual/spatial test places many children with AS at a distinct disadvantage. If some children have weaker spatial abilities and a spatial test is all that is given, then more representative ability measures are needed.

The purpose of cognitive assessment in children with autism is not necessarily to identify IQ scores, but to aide in identifying strengths and weaknesses so as to find the most appropriate modalities for promoting abstraction, memory, and other functions directly connected to classroom instruction and life-skills tasks.

The purpose of cognitive assessment in children with autism is not necessarily to identify IQ scores, but to aide in identifying strengths and weaknesses so as to find the most appropriate modalities for promoting abstraction, memory, and other functions directly connected to classroom instruction and life-skills tasks. Multiple tests or test sections may be required to check the same targeted assessed skill. The examiner should always use multiple assessment measures when assessing a child suspected of having AS or autism, because one test alone does not always have sufficient power to determine a diagnosis.

It is important to remember that a diagnosis or general working knowledge of a child with AS or suspected of having AS should not be made by rating scales alone. A comprehensive psychological assessment is required. The word *comprehensive* should not be interpreted to mean that every available, relevant test should be administered. In a psychological assessment, you must depend on the professional judgment of the licensed or certified psychologist, using the current knowledge about AS and his or her experience with the child. The following procedures would be expected in a thorough assessment, given that the assessment in question is not a reevaluation of a child with whom a psychologist is not familiar:

1. A thorough medical, family, birth, developmental, and educational history from record reviews.
2. Direct face-to-face parent interview(s).
3. Careful clinical observations of the parent-child interaction.
4. Interviews with current school staff, which might include regular education teachers, special education teachers, and related service providers, such as speech pathologists, counselors, and occupational and physical therapists.
5. Telephone interview with physician, psychiatrist, or private therapist as needed.
6. Meaningful classroom observation(s).
7. Interview with student prior to testing.
8. A measure of visual-motor graphic skills with a writing implement, such as a writing sample and completion of the Beery-Buktenica Development Test of Visual-Motor Integration or the Rey-Osterrieth Complex Figure Test. A human figure drawing may also have clinical utility.
9. A measure of independent adaptive skills like the Vineland Adaptive Behavior Scales, Second Edition (Vineland-II), or the Woodcock-Johnson Scales of Independent Behavior (SIB).
10. An IQ test or relevant clusters or indexes from more than one IQ test.
11. Rating scales of attention, such as the Conners Rating Scales–Revised or the ADHD Rating Scale–IV.
12. Ratings of executive functioning, such as the Behavior Rating Inventory of Executive Functioning (BRIEF).

13. Ratings of behavior and psychopathology, such as Behavior Assessment System for Children, Second Edition (BASC-2).
14. Self-ratings of self-esteem, such as the Piers-Harris–II Self-Concept Scale.
15. A measure of social skills, such as the Social Skills Rating System.
16. Self-ratings of depression and anxiety, such as the Reynolds scales or the BASC-2.
17. Measures of obsessive and compulsive behaviors, such as the Yale-Brown Obsessive Compulsive Scale (Y-BOCS).
18. Projective tests of distortion of perception or illogical thinking, such as projective stories or the Rorschach Inkblot Test.

The above list of assessment tools is not a mandatory battery or necessarily comprehensive, but simply a listing of the kinds of procedures that a responsible clinical or school psychologist who is certified or licensed might employ to aide in his or her decision making in a diagnosis of AS.

As research evidence continues to build, a pattern seems to be emerging. AS is an autistic disorder because of poor reciprocity skills, but fits uniquely in its own category due to pedantic speech, preoccupation with restricted topics of interest, general verbal strengths with poor pragmatic skills, sensory sensitivities, and motor awkwardness. In the next chapter, we will discuss some of the additional aspects of AS, ones that may present themselves more readily to parents and teachers.

chapter 4

Additional Aspects of AS

IN so many ways, Juan was a wonderful student. He generally participated in class, even if he was a little quirky and sometimes said the things that other kids were thinking, but wouldn't say out loud. He could write at length about the facts of any assignment, which usually was enough to help him get good grades, even in his high school Honors classes. Only when you saw the symptoms of his AS would you realize the significance of his challenges. These challenges might occur at odd or infrequent times. Even as a high school student, he was alarmed by loud, unpredictable noises, such as the fire alarm, and would put his fingers in his ears and get very agitated when these occurred. Although interested in sports, Juan would never go to a game, because of the high levels of noise and confusion. The social scene of high school, especially as it related to interactions with the opposite sex, baffled him and he avoided it. Although he could write volumes about the facts of any topic, he had great difficulty when called on to talk about the motivation of the characters or to explain how he arrived at an answer in math or science. Due to his clumsiness and his discomfort in large groups, he needed to take weight training every semester, rather than participate with the other students in the regular physical education classes. Juan was an excellent student in many ways, but was still greatly affected by AS.

In Chapter 3, we presented the pivotal aspects of AS used to form a diagnosis. However, parents and teachers are likely to notice many other aspects of AS that may impact development and learning. In this chapter, we will describe the features of this syndrome that are frequently encountered by parents and teachers.

Sensory and Motor Concerns

Although clumsiness has been described as a feature of AS, Ghaziuddin, Tsai, and Ghaziuddin (1992) have pointed out that these weaknesses needed to be more universally defined. A research project by Green and colleagues (2002) demonstrated that significant motor impairments were found on all 11 students with AS in their study as measured by two standardized measures. Dunn, Myles, and Orr (2002) used a sample size of 42 children with AS and found clear differences in sensory processing as compared to peers without disabilities. Sensory issues have been found in a few studies to be highly correlated with emotional reactivity (Myles et al., 2004), especially anxiety and sensory defensiveness (Pfeiffer, 2004).

Hooper, Poon, Marcus, and Fine (2006) have found that dynamic balance and diadochokinesis (alternating hand and limb movements) were impaired in children and adolescents with AS when compared to neurotypical children. Children with AS often suffer from hypotonia or the lack of good muscle tone. Fitness and exercise programs are often utilized as part of physical therapy treatment for such children.

One of the most common overall problems in AS and most forms of autism is sensory integration dysfunction; in other words, the inability to pull together perceptions, proprioceptive movements (internal signals from muscle movements and positions), and motor responses into an integrated whole. The oft-cited clumsiness and hyper- and hyposensitivity to stimuli in the environment represent examples of difficulties in this area. Also, the great majority of students with AS have motor problems that affect graphomotor aspects of written expression, such as handwriting.

Multiple treatment modalities and methods are used by occupational and physical therapists in direct treatment through pull-out programs, during instruction in the classroom, or in consultation with special and regular education teachers. A thorough description of sensory integration issues, as well as many appropriate suggestions for dealing with these issues, are included in the book *The Out of Sync Child* (Kranowitz & Miller, 2005).

Attention Problems

Although full-blown ADHD often is not found to accompany AS, attention problems are linked to AS. The nature of the disability as a variation of autism includes the problem of not knowing what is salient or what is important to attend to. Therefore, people with AS may have difficulty identifying the critical, pivotal elements in a perceptual array. They may attend to the wrong things. Through a small sample study, Rogers (2000) found that teens and young adults failed to hierarchically place proper special status on key stimuli. On the motor side, Rinehart, Bradshaw, Brereton, and Tonge (2001) discovered that children with AS did not properly prepare to execute a motor response, but had the ability to perform the response.

Children with AS may not pay attention to what their parent or teacher require. Also, they may demonstrate an attention drift, where they may periodically "space out" or become disconnected from ongoing situations. Schatz, Weimer, and Trauner (2002) found evidence of attention deficits through a computerized test in the majority of their subjects. Tani et al. (2006) found that a majority of a small sample of 20 adults in a retrospective rating of ADHD symptoms had significant scores on measures of inattention and hyperactivity in their childhoods. ADHD and attention problems are very frequently found in records of the early childhoods and classroom behavior of the clients we have reviewed.

Working Memory

There is evidence to suggest that persons with AS find it harder to maintain the same amount of information in their working memory than others. Working memory is used as you try to remember a phone number while you search for a pen to write it down. So, while they can admit a great deal of information in long-term memory, children with AS lack the ability to store short pieces of information, especially information unrelated to their central interests. Musarra (2006) reported a study of 30 boys diagnosed with AS who were tested with the Working Memory Test Battery for Children. The results supported the idea that working memory is a specific information processing deficit in persons with AS.

Executive Functions

Executive functions difficulties were first isolated conceptually as a group by Dr. Martha Denckla, director of the Developmental Cognitive Neurology Clinic at the Kennedy Krieger Institute in Baltimore, MD. She defined characteristics of executive functioning to include interference control, effortful and flexible organization, and strategic planning, or anticipatory goal-directed preparedness to act (Denckla, 1994). She also included working memory in this category. When there is dysfunction in the executive functions, Denckla (1994) claimed it occurs within the infrastructure she referred to as ISIS, or actions that require a person to Initiate, Sustain, Inhibit, and Shift attention and action. Much of the activity of executive functions, including planning, is thought to involve the prefrontal areas of the brain. Many children with AS tend to live very much in the immediate present and lack the ability to internalize a future context to plan and organize their actions. For example, a teenager may purchase a gift for a birthday party and not consider gathering the wrapping materials for the present, the birthday card, or the directions to the event, when there are only 30 minutes before she has to leave for the party.

Pace

Children with AS may cause some concern for teachers because their pace of doing classroom tasks might be slower than others. They have difficulty with speeded, timed, or hurried tasks. Often the student doesn't understand that the clock is ticking and there is an impending deadline. It is also likely that kids with AS may not have the same sense of internal time monitoring or subjective time as other kids.

In children with AS, the internal pace of decision making may be slowed along with consciousness of when it is important to be efficient or to hurry. It is also possible that the idea of rushing or adjusting one's pace to conditions or to demands of others is not that important to persons with AS. Therefore, they are not necessarily inclined to memorize, respond to, or sort information in an efficient manner.

Self-Reflection

Self-reflection is the general capacity that humans have to evaluate their behavior. This may be based on internal standards, acquired or otherwise, through adjusting behavior by modeling others. Self-reflection is a kind of feedback system based on learned external consequences of behavior, especially as these behaviors involve comparing one's own behavior to a standard. Most neurotypical people are constantly adjusting and evaluating their successes and failures to improve their effectiveness through feedback and internal language. People with AS may not have the same kind of internal language.

In our experience, many children with AS, if not most, tend not to be aware that they have a problem or are not able to accept that they do. There may be a core problem in AS and autism in general in terms of typical human self-reflective capacity. This may mean that persons with AS tend to have less-developed self-concepts or means for using feedback to regulate self-evaluation and self-esteem.

In our experience, many children with AS, if not most, tend not to be aware that they have a problem or are not able to accept that they do.

Self-concept may include the entire range of the internal view of one's self or general ways of seeing oneself instead of action-by-action trial and error. We may, however, have many self-concepts based upon our roles as brothers, sisters, friends, and others as pointed out by the great American psychologist and philosopher, William James (1890/1950). We may generalize a self-concept based upon how good we are at one particular area of skills, or we may simply have self-concept internal language about where we stand in our community. This reflects how we present ourselves and how others might see us. Because of a lack of development of these internal self-evaluation processes, a person with AS may not care about appearances. This might be reflected by her lack of awareness of basic prevailing fashion, so that she doesn't know how to dress or may represent herself in a manner that is far off base by adopting unusual clothing. She may try and fail at being "cool."

Self-esteem generally refers to the positive or negative value one places on one's behavior or any part of or the whole self. This is how we evaluate our performance of roles and responsibilities. Self-esteem in persons with AS can be very brittle. After experiencing continuing failures at attempting to communicate and adapt, a person with AS, especially if the syndrome is undiagnosed and/or unsupported, may have very low self-esteem. Thus, it is very important to identify AS as early as possible so as to nurture the person's self-esteem within the context and general understanding of his or her challenges.

Face Perception

Problems with emotional development may start with suspected weaknesses in facial perception. Klin, Jones, Schultz, Volkmar, and Cohen (2002), along with other researchers, have been using eye-tracking technology to record where autistic subjects are looking when various stimuli are presented. In one study, autistic subjects did not look at a human's eyes or body movements and normal controls did. In these initial studies, the eye movements of persons with AS were found to be tentative and unpredictable, and often focused on irrelevant objects away from the center of the frame. It is interesting to note that not all scanning is weaker in persons with autism. Shah and Frith (1983) reported better identification of a figure embedded in another visual pattern in autistic persons. Joliffe and Baron-Cohen (1997) also found stronger results in identifying embedded figures in drawings among autistic adults and those with AS over normal controls. We have seen this in some informal observations of children with "Where's Waldo" style puzzle books. Students with autism may seem to be unaffected and, therefore, not slowed by distractions familiar to other children, so that they are able to quickly identify target stimuli.

Some researchers argue that facial recognition and attributes of facial expressions are deficient in AS. This does not just include the ability to track facial activity. Deruelle, Rondan, Gepner, and Tardif (2004) demonstrated weaknesses in all aspects of face processing except the ability to match faces in subjects with AS compared to normal subjects. That included identification of emotions, direction of eye gaze, gender identification, and lip reading tasks. Autistic subjects did better when there was more local than global information in the face. This reinforces the importance of richly contextualizing information for autistic children when instructing them, so they can build knowledge. When teaching a new concept, it is highly beneficial for the teacher to tie it in with previously established knowledge associated with the concept. This is in concert with Temple Grandin's idea that images are saved in the autistic person's memory from small parts to the whole. They do not remember gestalts or whole, global forms as well as they do by building them with small parts. For example, a science teacher might teach the makeup of a cell by using a picture of the whole cell with each of the parts labeled when talking about the nucleus.

Baron-Cohen, Baldwin, and Crowson (1997) demonstrated that the discrimination of facial patterns and movements associated with simple emotions are significantly less developed in persons with AS than normal controls. Magnetic Resonance Imaging (MRI) techniques have been used to demonstrate that there is decreased activation of one part of the brain (fusiform gyrus) in autistic subjects during face processing (Pierce & Courchesne, 2000). It is as if some brain areas are less developed, wired, or networked to perform this function. Grossman, Klin, Carter, and Volkmar (2000) suggested that persons with AS may use visual-verbal over visual-emotional associations to compensate for the lack of ability to process emotional information. This is consistent with Temple Grandin's (1995) "thinking in pictures" activity, in which memories are stored through categories in internally visualized pictures.

There is a neurological disorder called prosopagnosia that refers to the inability to recognize faces. Barton and colleagues (2004) reported on a study that proved that this is not the case with persons with AS. It is most likely the emotional and social-cue laden configurations and movements of the face that are poorly discriminated. A similar finding by Hefter, Manoach, and Barton (2005) led the researchers to conclude that the results of their study argued against the idea that social dysfunction in social developmental disorders causes a generalized failure to acquire face-processing skills. They suggest that processing of emotions causes face-processing problems and not the other way around. A recent study by White, Hill, Winston, and Frith (2006) demonstrated that not all aspects of social knowledge are compromised in AS. Some weaknesses in facial processing may be related to the problems in being able to take another person's point of view. It appears clear that people with AS, particularly males, have greater difficulty in recognizing emotion from faces than voices (Golan, Baron-Cohen, & Hill, 2006). Instructionally, this suggests that human voice features of emotion can be utilized in a dramatic fashion and modeled as a good instructional process. We were able to deduce this when observing highly regarded teachers of children with AS who utilize dramatic gesture and voice emphasis during instruction. A study by Fitzgerald and Bellgrove (2006) demonstrated that persons with AS have alexithymia, or the reduced ability to express emotions verbally. We recognize this from the monotonic, and often pedantic, rigidity in verbal expression in many persons with AS. Emotional processing in persons with AS, then, is an input and output problem.

Reinforcing this idea, a recent study (Hubert et al., in press) demonstrated that interpretation of whole-body movements portrayed by points of light were weaker in persons with AS than controls. So, the interpretation of emotion through facial expressions, as well as body postures and movements, is challenging for persons with AS. This is consistent with a very interesting study conducted by Castelli and colleagues in 2002, who compared interpretation of animated geometric shapes between persons with autism and AS and persons considered to be neurotypical controls. The autism group showed less activation on a PET scan than normal controls. Normal controls attributed human actions and motives to the movement of the shapes, as one would interpret the relationships between cartoon characters. During the scan, the autistic and AS subjects did not attribute human actions and emotions to the movement of the shapes.

Computerized methods are arising to train or retrain face processing. One such study (Silver & Oakes, 2001) used a program called the "Emotion Trainer," which has been developed to help autistic individuals recognize and predict emotional responses of others. Repetition with such techniques appears to show promise in initial test results. "Let's Face It" is a program developed by Tanaka, Lincoln, and Hegg (2003) that develops a child's learning of facial expressions. Baron-Cohen and Wheelwright (2003) used a test called Reading the Mind in the Eyes to detect subtle individual differences in social sensitivity in adults with AS. This test involves choosing descriptive labels for the emotions expressed through pictures of eyes.

Emotional Development

Depression not only may be an inherited emotional tendency in persons with AS, but may be a result of the experience of frustration and failure in reacting or interacting effectively with the world, especially in interacting successfully with other people.

Depression not only may be an inherited emotional tendency in persons with AS, but may be a result of the experience of frustration and failure in reacting or interacting effectively with the world, especially in interacting successfully with other people. Every person has a general temperament and moods, such as excitability versus calmness, ease with others or shyness, and slowness to anger versus irritability and explosiveness. For example, some people are more or less subject to sadness. Sadness may not last as long with some people than others or may be pervasively experienced throughout the day or almost every day with some people, but rarely experienced in others. Not only are there mood regulation differences, but some people inherit a tendency to lifelong depression (unipolar) or have a rare mood disorder, bipolar depression, characterized by a manic phase, as well. Currently bipolar depression is highly overdiagnosed and misunderstood. Psychiatrist David Behar, M.D., in a letter to *Clinical Psychiatric News* (1998) described bipolar disorder as being "absurdly over diagnosed." He added, "Any overreacting patient now gets the label and a mood stabilizer" (Behar, 1998, p. 20). The problem generally occurs during periods of time (often found in adolescence) when there are great changes in emotional experience, or when life is on a "roller-coaster." Still, it is very important to distinguish between general ups and downs in moods and bipolar disorder, which has a very distinct collection of symptoms (American Psychiatric Association, 1994).

The sum total of temperament, personality, moods, and habits, including conformance to communally held and internalized ethical standards, is called *character*. Emotional issues are frequently part of a package of coexisting conditions referred to by mental health professionals as *comorbid symptoms*. In order to avoid the unpleasant stigmatizing value attached to this term, we choose to use the term *coexisting*. Gillberg (2003) has provided a clinical analysis of autism and AS and how they coexist with other disorders in childhood. For example, attention problems are among the most noticed coexisting conditions in childhood (Lee & Ousley, 2006).

Anxiety and depression are probably the most frequently observed coexisting condition with AS in adulthood. Quite frequently, the rigidity and fear of novelty in persons with AS result in their feeling overwhelmed with too many new experiences or unexpected situations. This leaves them in a state of apprehension about what might happen resulting from their lack of ability to predict or control situations. A more common problem than depression in early development is spiraling anxiety, or the buildup of apprehension that comes from anticipation of complexity or failure, or both. Anxiety can become incapacitating, and persons with AS can shut down and become angry because they simply are on overload and can't cope. One of the results of this emotional overload is what appear to be paranoid symptoms. It is not surprising that when people with AS develop mistrust and attribute ill will to others, they can be confused with persons with paranoid personality disorders or paranoid psychosis. A study by Craig, Hatton, Craig, and Bentall (2004) demonstrated a difference between low-level paranoid symptoms in persons with AS and the delusions found in psychotic paranoia. Paranoid persons with psychosis tended to make more external personal attribution to others for negative events. There are less attribution abnormalities in persons with AS. Despite this fact, paranoid symptoms can be diagnostically overvalued in the emergency psychiatric setting when adults have gotten into trouble. There is a chance that adults with AS can be misidentified as psychotic (Raja & Azzoni, 2001).

Persons with AS usually find social exchanges to be frustrating, because they require flexibility in responding to different contexts and cues. This is severely limited by rigidity. This might reflect the person's neurological limitations in handling novelty at all levels. The result may be low self-esteem and depression. Myles and Southwick's (1999) book, *Asperger Syndrome and Difficult Moments: Practical Solutions for Tantrums, Rage, and Meltdowns*, covers a number of specific strategies for de-escalating emotional reactions in children with AS when the reactions become out of control. Without regard to the neurological bases of emotional problems in the lives of persons with AS, it is clear that many behavioral and emotional issues stem from problems in personal stress management. Myles and Southwick (1999) note that many children and youth with AS exhibit anxiety, which, under stress, can escalate into challenging behaviors. These behaviors need to be viewed, at times, as part of the condition. It is important to understand the cycle of behaviors to prevent seemingly minor events from escalating and spiraling. Myles points out that positive behavior change will not occur unless the function of the behavior is understood and the student is provided instruction and support in using (a) strategies that increase social understanding and problem solving, (b) techniques that facilitate self-understanding, and (c) methods of self-calming (Myles & Southwick, 1999).

Social/emotional issues may emerge at differing times in the life of the student with AS. For example, middle school is a potentially very turbulent period. From a hormonal, neurological, and general developmental perspective, no one can predict what an entering sixth grader will look like after finishing eighth grade. The amount of physical change in middle school is far greater than any other 3-year span of time in a person's life. This has significant implications for the needs for emotional support, the development of control over executive functions, and the modulation of anxiety, depression, irritability, and oppositional behavior that are generally found in any neurotypical child in early adolescence. Adolescent physical changes can play havoc on the emotional life of a child with AS.

The features of AS discussed above must be taken into consideration in parenting and the development of educational plans. The next three chapters will deal specifically with how AS may be appearing in the classroom and what interventions can be used to work effectively with these students.

chapter 5 Best Practices in School

SHAWN appears in his counselor's office during the second period of his first day in middle school. Overwhelmed with anxiety, he has wandered the school building, trying to find his classes. The noise of the hallways, with the hustle and bustle of movement between classes, has almost put him in a state of shock. It has been hard for him to formulate questions for other students or teachers to help him in finding his way. Trying to be strong, he holds back tears. He had already gotten upset as he left his first period class, where things had not gone well. Students had been called on to introduce themselves and tell about one area of interest. He didn't know why the teacher had insisted on cutting him off in the middle of his discussion of all of the Pokémon characters. Things had only gotten worse when all students were assigned to read a short passage and he was called on and asked to explain what the main character might have been thinking, before the climax of the story. He had no clue how to answer the question. The loud sounds of the practice fire drill only contributed more to his upset, and finally, he was completely thrown off when he packed up his books to go at 8:45 a.m., the ending time for the class listed on his schedule, only to be told that this was an extended first period for the first day of school. By the time Shawn found the counselor's office, his only desire was to return to the safe, predictable environment of his elementary school.

Dealing with the typical school environment may prove to be very difficult for the child or young adult with AS. He may find school to be a place that does not seem to value or utilize his personal strengths and where he is asked to deal with tasks and an environment that directly impacts his weaknesses or differences. Teachers may feel frustrated in trying to reach these students who are not able to perform when taught in the standard way, and they may feel that they don't have the expertise to provide the range of strategies and interventions that these students may require.

The next three chapters will explore how the attributes of AS are likely to appear in the school environment. A philosophy that has been successful in working with bright students with learning difficulties, including students with AS, will be presented. Specific strategies that have proven to be successful in dealing with each of the major characteristics of AS in the classroom will be outlined. In Chapter 6, tools that can be used by teachers, parents, and the students themselves will be presented to help students overcome their weaknesses. The focus on school strategies will conclude in Chapter 7 with a look at the range of school options that might appropriately serve students with AS and a discussion of how parents can effectively access these services and programs.

As discussed in previous chapters, teachers and parents may be frustrated to see a child who seems very capable in terms of his or her knowledge of specific topics and may be an advanced reader and/or strong in areas of math or science, but at the same time is unable to handle much of the higher level comprehension work of the classroom. The student may go on and on talking about his area of special interest, but be unable to write a coherent paragraph about the same topic. He may know the daily schedule better than the teacher, but get thrown off by any changes and startled by any sudden or unusual sound or event. She may be extremely orderly with her possessions or collections, but very disorganized when it comes to her school tasks.

. . . teachers and parents may be frustrated to see a child who seems very capable in terms of his or her knowledge . . . , but at the same time is unable to handle much of the higher level comprehension work of the classroom.

Of even greater concern may be the student's weaknesses in social interactions. This may be made more difficult by the individual's problems with understanding the subtleties of language and nonverbal communication, such as facial expressions or gestures. These difficulties with social interactions, which are especially evident within peer interactions, may be a source of the anxiety, low self-esteem, and depression that are prevalent in children with AS.

The following is a summary of the issues that teachers and parents are likely to observe in the classroom in students with AS. We will explore each of these areas and offer strategies for helping students to deal with these problems in greater detail in Chapter 6. The issues include:

- problems with social interactions;
- very focused areas of interest and expertise;
- need for predictability;
- problems with language;
- problems with abstract reasoning;

- problems with sensory hyper- or hyposensitivity;
- problems with anxiety, depression, and emotional regulation;
- problems with attention, organization, and other areas of executive functioning;
- problems with motor issues including written production; and
- problems with ritualistic, repetitive, or rigid behavior.

Before entering into our discussion of the strategies that have proven successful with each of the problem areas, it's important to have an overview of the best practices for working with smart kids with learning difficulties, including students who have AS. Four areas of best practices for working with bright students with learning difficulties in the classroom have been identified (Weinfeld, Barnes-Robinson, Jeweler, & Roffman Shevitz, 2006). The four major components are:

1. instruction in the student's area of strength;
2. opportunities for the instruction of skills and strategies in academic areas affected by the student's challenges;
3. an appropriately differentiated program including individualized instructional adaptations and accommodations systematically provided to students; and
4. comprehensive case management to coordinate all aspects of the student's individual educational plan. (Weinfeld et al., 2006, p. 62)

Best Practice 1: Instruction in the Student's Area of Strength

It is clear that if students are to succeed in life they will do so by capitalizing on their strengths. Temple Grandin is one example of an individual with Asperger's syndrome who has made use of her remarkable visual strengths to be a highly valued and productive member of society.

Schools must provide an opportunity for students to identify and build on their strengths, to learn how these strengths connect to careers, and to utilize their strengths to overcome their weaknesses. Adapting a lesson so that it capitalizes on the individual student's strengths allows all students to access the curriculum. Accommodating for students by allowing them to depend on their strengths allows the students to circumvent their weaknesses. When a student's strengths are recognized and utilized in the classroom, she sees that she is a respected and valued member of that classroom community.

Schools must provide an opportunity for students to identify and build on their strengths, to learn how these strengths connect to careers, and to utilize their strengths to overcome their weaknesses. . . . When a student's strengths are recognized and utilized in the classroom, she sees that she is a respected and valued member of that classroom community.

Some of the strengths that students with Asperger's typically display are a strong base of information, a large vocabulary, reading decoding ability, and visual-spatial strengths. As these strengths are developed, they can form the basis for a lifelong love of learning. When the student is assigned a specific role in a cooperative learning group that utilizes his strengths, he can express classroom success that builds true self-esteem and fosters social relationships.

Students with AS also frequently show a passion for learning and a desire to share their knowledge. Unfortunately, this passion and desire may be focused on a narrow area of interest or interests. By allowing time for the student to learn about and share his or her knowledge about this area of interest, the teacher is again promoting self-esteem, by showing the student that he or she belongs in the classroom and by gaining a valuable tool for managing the student's behavior. Over time, the teacher is also cultivating the opportunity for the student to expand and broaden his or her area of interest and to see how it may apply to a variety of new topics.

Best Practice 2: Opportunities for the Instruction of Skills and Strategies in Academic Areas Affected by the Student's Challenges

When the emphasis of the instruction is on the student's strengths, she will be much more willing to spend some time working on her areas of weakness. We owe it to the students in our classroom not to give up on developing all of their skills.

Although we believe in placing an emphasis on strength-based instruction, teachers and other school staff must also provide instruction in the skills and strategies that are challenging to the student with AS. When the emphasis of the instruction is on the students' strengths, she will be much more willing to spend some time working on her areas of weakness. We owe it to the students in our classroom not to give up on developing all of their skills. For the student with Asperger's, this means directly teaching him how to improve his social skills, as well as how to improve his ability to organize, attend to tasks, write effectively, comprehend advanced materials, and handle changes in his school environment. It's important to note that it is not just the classroom teacher, but also a team of individuals, including the counselor, speech pathologist, occupational therapist, the school psychologist, and the special education teacher, who are responsible for this instruction of skills and strategies.

Best Practice 3: An Appropriately Differentiated Program, Including Individualized Instructional Adaptations and Accommodations Systematically Provided to Students

Although we have the responsibility to teach students how to improve in their areas of weakness, we must recognize that many of the weaknesses that we see in each of these students are directly impacted by the fact that they have AS. Therefore, it is crucial that we provide the appropriate adaptations and accommodations that will allow these students to access the curriculum and utilize their strengths. Appropriately selected adaptations and accommodations make it possible for all students to function at their best and to not only have a level playing field, but to work toward realizing their potential. In choosing appropriate adaptations and accommodations, it is always crucial to remember that we are striving to move the student from dependence to independence over time. An accommodation such as having a student dictate her response to an adult may be very appropriate early in a student's educational career, but inappropriate when the same student has learned to utilize computer keyboards and organizational software. It is crucial that we measure the effectiveness of accommodations over time and either change or eliminate those that are not effective. Finally, it is crucial that all staff members who will work with the student understand the reason for the accommodation (Weinfeld et al., 2006). As students move from dependence to independence, they must be a crucial part of this process, understanding their own unique strengths and weaknesses and being able to be self-advocates.

Teachers who have learned about the principles of differentiation will be the most effective in working with this population of students (Tomlinson, 1999). These are the teachers who understand that within the same lesson, which contains the same goals for understanding, there are different ways for students to acquire the content. There are different learning activities that will engage different learners and different ways for students to demonstrate that they have learned the information. Teachers who understand this will provide the adaptations and accommodations students with AS need to be successful.

Best Practice 4: Comprehensive Case Management to Coordinate All Aspects of the Student's Individual Educational Plan

It is crucial that each student who has been identified as having AS have a case manager at school who is responsible for overseeing his or her program. Depending on the type of formal or informal plan that may be in place (see Chapter 7 for more information about types of plans), a special educator, the school counselor, or the classroom teacher may act as case manager. The case manager is responsible for making sure that the student is both being challenged appropriately and receiving the appropriate supports that will allow him to access the curriculum and be successful in school. The case manager coordinates all of the school's resources and communicates with all school staff about the student's needs. It is crucial that they develop a partnership with the home so that there is two-way communication between the parents and any involved community service providers and the school staff.

This team approach will allow for those who are working with the student to work together in the best interest of the student. The case manager makes sure that the student is part of their plan, helping to educate the team about his or her unique strengths, challenges, and the accommodations that he or she needs in order to be successful. When it is time to modify or create a new plan, typically on a yearly basis, it is the case manager who takes the lead on coordinating this process. Whenever possible, the student should be invited to be a full participant in the meeting. This may require coaching. When the goals or objectives are clear and simple and there is relative agreement among adults at the table, the student can benefit from being part of the process and taking ownership of his own progress.

Conclusion

Students with AS, like other bright kids with learning difficulties, can be successful in school when these four best practices are applied to their school experience. Parents and teachers must work together to find ways to utilize and develop the students' strengths; to teach them how to improve in their areas of weakness; to provide them with appropriate adaptations and accommodations that will allow them access to challenging instruction; and to provide case management that facilitates a strong team approach at school and a strong partnership between school and home. We will discuss strategies to do each of these things in the next few chapters.

chapter 6

Strategies and Interventions That Work in the Classroom

IN Montgomery County, MD's, public school district Asperger's program, the day begins with circle time. The student repeats that "it's important to use a lot of language," as he works on identifying the emotions in the picture of the face that the teacher is holding up. The teacher models excited emotions as she tells a personal story and each student attempts to emulate what she has demonstrated as they describe their own weekend experiences. The students work on keeping eye contact with each other as they take turns speaking. As the teacher refers to the visual schedule to preview the upcoming day, she prepares the students for the fact that today there will be an unscheduled surprise, and talks about how they will handle it. As she talks about the science lesson that will come up later in the day, she allows the students to talk briefly about their own independent exploration of their current topic of passion that they will have time to pursue as part of the day's lesson. It is clear that the students, despite their obvious difficulties with social communication, their difficulties with flexibility, and their own focused interests, are making great academic and social progress in this supportive environment.

In Chapter 5, we outlined the areas that provide the greatest challenge for teachers and for the students themselves. In this chapter, we will discuss the accommodations that have proven effective in the classroom for each of these issues. These accommodations have been drawn from many sources, as well as from our experience gained in years of working with students in a variety of school environments (Attwood, 1996; Klin et al., 2000; Magnusen & Attwood, 2005; Myles & Adreon, 2001; Powers & Poland, 2003; Ralabate, 2006; Weinfeld et al., 2006).

The 10 issues we will be discussing include:

- problems with social interactions;
- very focused areas of interest and expertise;
- need for predictability;
- problems with language;
- problems with abstract reasoning;
- problems with sensory hyper- or hyposensitivity;
- problems with anxiety, depression, and emotional regulation;
- problems with attention, organization, and other areas of executive functioning;
- problems with motor issues including written production; and
- problems with ritualistic, repetitive, or rigid behavior.

Each section that follows also provides specific strategies to help students with AS overcome these issues.

Problems With Social Interactions

Social interactions provide a challenge for students with AS. There may be more than one process operating in social skills deficits. On one level, there is the ability to recognize emotions through reading faces, body posture, and voice inflection, and on another, the ability to make good cognitive judgments using the data obtained from this reading. Johnson (2004) suggests that social deficits may be due to a lack of integration among various perceptual and higher level abilities, as well as social memory or recall. Although students with AS sometimes relate well to adults, especially when they are allowed to focus on their area of interest or expertise, they tend to have greater difficulties in relating to their peers. Adults may be unaware that they are unconsciously assisting the student with AS by keeping the conversation flowing. Teachers may see the social skills difficulties when students with AS are assigned to work cooperatively on an academic project.

These social challenges may be more evident during unstructured times such as transition times between activities or at lunch or recess. Even when the student's social problems primarily occur away from the classroom, they still may affect the student academically in that he may be preoccupied with the social interactions and may feel anxiety and/or sadness as a result of his problems with these interactions. Teachers also may see these students struggling with understanding the perspective, thoughts, and emotions of the characters in their assigned readings. Therefore, students with AS may struggle to answer comprehension questions that involve understanding the motivation of the characters in their classroom reading selections.

Strategies and Interventions That Work With Social Interactions

Protect Students From Bullying and Teasing

It is crucial that schools develop a policy with zero tolerance for bullying and teasing.

Teachers and school administrators must create a safe environment for students with AS. It is crucial that schools develop a policy with zero tolerance for bullying and teasing. Schools that have education programs that proactively educate all students about bullying and teasing have been the most effective in establishing a climate that is safe for all students (Suckling & Temple, 2001). Anti-bullying programs increase in effectiveness when included in school policies that promote positive citizenship in general. There should be an established procedure for reporting and dealing with any incidents of bullying and teasing that do arise. It is imperative that the role of the "victim," a role in which students with AS often find themselves, is explored and that the victim is given help with strategies he can use to proactively avoid the bullying or teasing (Neu & Weinfeld, 2006).

The Medina City Schools (located in Ohio) program for students with AS will be highlighted in Chapter 10. They have had great success teaching a social skills program utilizing the Super Skills program developed by Judith Coucouvanis (2005) as a guide. Super Skills presents 30 lessons grouped under four types of social skills: fundamental skills, social initiation skills, getting along with others, and social response skills. In addition to highly structured, easy-to-follow lessons, the book offers a series of practical checklists and other instruments to provide a solid foundation for assessing students' social skills levels and doing subsequent planning.

Educate Other Students About AS and About the Child's Unique Strengths and Challenges

By educating classmates and schoolmates about the challenges of the individual child, a climate of understanding and support can be cultivated. The school counselor or psychologist may take the lead on this education and be able to present information in a way that is age appropriate. At older ages, the student with Asperger's may self-advocate, as she helps educate her classmates about her own strengths, challenges, and needs.

Utilize Strengths and Interests in Cooperative Learning

Teachers can help students to be successful in group learning situations by defining the student's role in the group so that she can utilize her strengths. When they are given the task of remembering facts for the group, students with AS can serve as valuable and positive members of a group learning activity. Similarly, their strong reliance on routine may help them to take on leadership roles in remembering the steps of the group task. Especially in the elementary grades, they may be the most skilled group members when it comes to reading aloud or demonstrating understanding of advanced vocabulary. Teachers also can set the stage for positive and valued contributions to the group if there is a structured expectation for the student to share an area of personal interest or expertise that helps the group toward its common goal. Conversely, the teacher will need to structure the group setting so that the student with AS is not expected to socialize with others in a way beyond her current ability. Teachers can scaffold these social interactions by providing the student who has AS with some questions he should ask of the other students.

Rehearsal of group work time and utilization of social stories that help the student to learn about the expectations of the group work time are also valuable ways to prepare for this potentially difficult situation. The social stories method was first developed by Carol Gray in 1991 and periodically has been modified and updated since that time (Gray & White, 2002). Social stories present appropriate social behaviors in the form of a story in an effort to help students with AS learn how to deal with a variety of situations. The stories include descriptive sentences that describe what people do, perspective sentences that describe typical reactions to the situation, directive sentences that direct the person to the appropriate response, and control sentences that help the person with AS to remember to use what he or she has learned in the social story when the challenging situation arises. Gray and White emphasize that for every control or directive sentence, there should be two to five descriptive and prescriptive sentences. Students with AS need to be taught social skills, such as reading social cues and using coping strategies, in an emotionally safe environment (Marks et al., 1999).

Teach Theory of Mind: Learning to Understand the Perspectives, Feelings, and Thoughts of Others

Students with AS tend to have great difficulty taking on the perspective of another person. They need to be explicitly taught how neurotypical people think. This should be done in a way that communicates that there's not anything wrong with the way that the child with Asperger's thinks. As Dr. Michael McManmon, the founder and executive director of the College Internship Program says, "We teach our students that they are like Apple computers, when the rest of the world is PC" (M. McManmon, personal communication, December 2006). Dr. McManmon and his staff emphasize to their students that there's nothing wrong with Apple computers, but because most of the rest of the world has a different operating system, the Apple computers need to be able to communicate with the other operating system. The College Internship Program is located in several cities across the United States and provides comprehensive supports to students with AS, as well as other disabilities, so that they can be successful in taking part in the programs of the neighboring college campuses.

Similarly, students with AS need to be encouraged to stop and think about how the neurotypical student will feel before they speak or act. Again, it may be the school psychologist, counselor, or speech pathologist who takes the lead in educating the student about theory of mind, but the classroom teacher certainly can support this effort by explaining his or her thinking and asking students to do the same.

Teach Students How to Read and React to Nonverbal Social Cues

Students with AS need to be explicitly taught how to read nonverbal gestures and communication. They need to be taught about appropriate personal space and about facial expressions and gestures that signal interest or lack of interest. They need to be able to link facial expressions with the variety of emotions that they represent. Students with AS can be taught to remember a time that they felt like the emotion that the facial expression or gesture illustrates. They can be taught to link the feelings represented nonverbally with movies, cartoons, or books that illustrate that emotion. Similarly, they can be taught to identify and label the purpose of the nonverbal gesture that is used by neurotypical peers to regulate social interaction. One outstanding resource is a DVD called *Mind Reading,* developed in 2004 by Dr. Simon Baron-Cohen at Cambridge University, that uses video clips to teach students to identify emotions in others.

Teach Students How to Participate in Conversations

Students with AS do not have difficulty reading only nonverbal social clues—they also frequently have difficulties understanding the rules of conversation. Again, they need explicit instruction to help them learn these rules. Specifically, these students need to be taught how to enter a conversation, shift topics, expand on a topic, and repair breakdowns in conversations by seeking clarification or assistance when confused. The following are conversational skill areas for instruction:

- introductions,
- greetings,
- goodbyes,
- eye contact,
- turn-taking,
- volume,
- humor,
- requesting,
- protesting,
- giving approval,
- stating disapproval,
- explaining,
- organization of social exchanges,
- teamwork,
- courtesy words, and
- good sportsmanship.

Students with AS especially need help with how to participate in a conversation on a topic of interest to another person that does not interest them. There are a variety of approaches to teach this skill. Students explicitly can be taught about the qualities of a "good friend." They also can be taught to observe other children to indicate what they should do. There are many different materials available for teaching social skills. A few social skills programs that have been observed to be particularly effective with students with AS are Super Skills by Judith Coucouvanis, Building Social Relationships: A Systematic

Approach to Teaching Social Interaction Skills to Children and Adolescents With Autism Spectrum Disorders and Other Social Difficulties by Scott Bellini, and Thinking of You Thinking of Me by Michelle Garcia Winner (B. Myles, personal communication, February 2007).

The Online Asperger Syndrome Information and Support (OASIS) Web site (http://www.aspergersyndrome.com) lists many valuable resources for the teaching of social skills, as well as for other issues related to AS. Students with AS can be taught social skills through dramatizing or roleplaying a conversation, viewing or creating a comic strip conversation that provides a visual representation, or listening to or writing a social story that features the appropriate interactions (Gray & White, 2002). Coaching is required to avoid these problems and correct mistakes. Traditional talking psychotherapies alone will not be as effective as a very practical coaching approach. Research on the social interactions of a small group of teenagers with AS in Australia by Carrington, Templeton, and Papinczak (2003) found themes in their data, mainly (a) understanding of concepts or language regarding friends, (b) description of what is a friend, (c) description of what is not a friend, (d) description of an acquaintance, and (e) using masquerading to cope with social deficits. Many students with AS struggle with social interaction. One social interaction behavioral learning strategy is SODA, which stands for Stop, Observe, Deliberate, and Act (Bock, 2001). Using the acronym SODA to help them remember the steps, students are taught to stop and analyze possible responses before reflexively responding in social situations.

To date, there is no single model treatment program for social skills deficits in persons with AS (Kiker, 2006). Solomon, Goodlin-Jones, and Anders (2004) reported a 20-week social adjustment enhancement curriculum for boys aged 8–12. Target areas addressed were emotion recognition and understanding, theory of mind, and executive functions/real-life problem solving. This program included assessments of parents and concurrent training sessions for parents while the students received treatment. Depression scores decreased for less cognitively able and older boys. Maternal depression scores decreased and child behavior problems were reported less frequently. Social programs are one of the most frequently prescribed activities for children with AS, but outcome studies are needed to show what works. Development is often monitored with respect to peer interactions. Marriage, Gordon, and Brand (1995) reported on a social skills group program for eight boys with AS conducted weekly for 14 sessions. At the end of the study, the participants continued to engage more readily with the three therapists than with each other. The skills in the group did not generalize well to the home, school, or community setting. This suggests that supports for these children need to be monitored, supervised, and reinforced over a protracted period of time until the social skills are established or improved.

Conversely, students with AS also need to be taught that when they desire solitude there is a way that they can have it without offending others. Again, teachers can support this learning by discussing and modeling appropriate behavior in the classroom. It may be the counselor, psychologist, or speech pathologist who takes the lead in teaching these skills, whether they are taught individually or in social skills groups. Social skills or friendship groups may be comprised solely of students who need these supports or may be a combination of students with AS and their neurotypical peers. These groups can provide an opportunity to roleplay or rehearse social interactions. Even less formally, a peer or a group of peers may take on the task of helping the student learn more appropriate interactions. This type of group has been described as a "circle of friends," and is described in more detail on the OASIS Web site (http://www.asperger syndrome.com). Students with AS can be taught to decrease their inappropriate statements to others by learning to whisper their thoughts or to "think it, don't say it." When things do go wrong, a social autopsy can analyze the problem and try to come up with a general rule for future situations.

Teach Students to Identify and Understand Emotions

Underlying the problems with social interaction for many students with AS is an understanding of emotions. Students with AS can be taught to understand emotions by exploring one emotion at a time. Students can be taught to read and respond to the cues that indicate different levels of emotion and to use their visual skills to chart their own and others' emotions on a gauge. Teachers can support this learning by using language arts lessons to explore how the character in the story, poem, or autobiography may be feeling and why. Students may also respond to journaling about their feelings if they are provided with leading or guiding questions. Students with AS can be taught to learn and apply feeling labels.

Very Focused Areas of Interest and Expertise

Students with AS have very focused areas of interest and expertise. Although these may change over time, at any given time these students tend to be fixated on one or two particular topics. They often develop tremendous knowledge and expertise regarding their topic of expertise. They have a strong desire to read, hear, or view both additional information and the information that they are already familiar with about the chosen topic. They also are anxious to tell others what they know about the topic. Teachers may see this focused interest as a distraction from the concepts that the teacher wants to present on any given day. Teachers also may see the student with AS as disruptive to others, as he or she insists on discussing his or her topic of choice. On the other hand, when the student with AS is engaged in studying her topic of choice she is at her best as a focused,

When the student with AS is engaged in studying her topic of choice she is at her best as a focused, productive student.

productive student. When she is discussing her topic of choice she is engaged in talking to another person. It is also important for teachers to note that when the AS student is involved in reviewing or learning new information about her topic of choice, her classroom behavior may be at its best.

Strategies and Interventions That Work With Very Focused Areas of Interest and Expertise

Returning to our strength-based instruction model, presented in Chapter 5, it is crucial that classroom teachers recognize, respect, and value the student's area of interest and expertise. This area of focus can become a source of pride for the student, as he may, indeed, be the foremost expert on this area in his classroom. When the student can see that there is a respect and value for her area of interest, her overall motivation in the classroom may improve. Again, it is important to note that development of the student's passion for a particular topic and knowledge about that topic may eventually lead to that topic being a major in college and/or a source of employment (Grandin & Duffy, 2004)

Provide a Specific Time of the Day for Focus on the Area of Interest

Teachers can demonstrate their respect for and recognition of the student's special interest by providing a specific time of the day for the student to focus on this area. This scheduling not only provides recognition of the student's need to address his area of expertise, it can also help the student with AS to realize that other times of the day are not designated for that special interest. Teachers should communicate both the respect for the special interest area and clear expectations about the need to do work not related to the interest.

Help Students Develop Their Area of Interest and Relate It to Future Employment

Teachers can help a student to develop his passion by helping him explore the importance of his interest area, including the careers that are related to it. A guest speaker or a field trip to a related place of employment can have very special meaning for the individual student. Finding an adult mentor with a similar passion can also help the student see that her current interest can connect to a future career. On the other hand, for some students, their area of interest may be something that is not related to a career, but is a personal interest that is just for fun and may form the basis for a lifelong hobby.

Use the Special Area of Interest as a Bridge to Other Topics

Teachers can use the special area of interest as a bridge to other topics. A skillful teacher will find ways to relate other subject matter to the preferred topic. Similarly, teachers can gradually introduce related subtopics that expand the student's area of focus. Students with AS first may be asked to look at the differences and similarities in the related subtopic or subject of study. Teachers may use the student's area of interest as the basis for learning good research practices.

Use the Area of Interest as a Way to Facilitate Social Interaction

Counselors and teachers also can use the focused area of interest as a bridge to help the student with AS connect with peers who may have similar interests. The special area of focus can become a way to facilitate conversation and relationships among these peers. It may also help the student to develop social interactions through the Internet as he joins an existing chat room or builds his own chat room or Web site devoted to his interest.

Use the Student's Area of Interest to Help Regulate Behavior

Finally, school staff can use the student's interest area as a way to help him regulate his behavior. Regulated permission to read his book of interest, view his special video, or talk about his topic of passion will help the student with AS to relax and regain his composure during times when he may be feeling anxious, stressed, or depressed.

Need for Predictability

Teachers will see that any change in routine may be unsettling and upsetting to the student with AS. Students with AS need predictability and structure in their environment. This predictability applies to issues of time, rules and consequences, location, and who will be doing what. It is crucial that students with AS know what to expect and be given tools for handling any unforeseen, yet inevitable changes.

Strategies and Interventions That Work to Provide Predictability

An effective teacher of students with AS will strive to provide a predictable environment that includes clear rules and consequences.

Provide Clear Rules and Consequences

An effective teacher of students with AS will strive to provide a predictable environment that includes clear rules and consequences. Visual reminders and reinforcement tend to be especially important to students with AS. In terms of the rules and consequences of the classroom, the student with AS needs to have a visual reminder available. It may be helpful to have picture symbols accompanying words. For some students, having their own behavioral checklist or visual system may be particularly effective. A visual warning system, such as green, yellow, and red lights, may be a particularly effective way of communicating to the student how his behavior is appearing to the teacher. As mentioned previously, the student may also keep his own chart that visually monitors or gauges his emotional state. Visual organizers work for both behavior and academic support because visual/spatial skills are often strong in students with AS. They also work because something that is visual is predictable. It remains consistent and constant and does not change until it is replaced with a different visual organizer (Myles & Southwick, 1999).

When the student sees more than one teacher during the day, it is crucial that she understands the different rules and expectations of each teacher and has an easy reference to this variety of rules. Having consistency among the rules of different teachers will be a significant help to the student with AS.

Provide Clear Physical Structure in the Classroom

Students with AS will respond best to a classroom that is clearly labeled with the locations of materials, the location of activities, and clearly posted information that includes both rules and directions. The predictability that this structure will bring to the classroom provides students with AS the organizational supports they need and decreases their anxiety. As stated earlier, having things clearly labeled ensures that the student with AS can be sure that these structures will not change.

Provide a Clear Physical Schedule in the Classroom

Because students with AS depend on the consistency of routines, it is crucial that they know the schedule for the day. They will respond best to a visual schedule. It is even better if the visual schedule is also provided for them individually. For example, the instructor may support the student's maintenance of a personal calendar. A personal calendar in the student's possession provides security as an organizational reference tool and as a ready reference source. This may be in electronic form as an organizer program on a computer or a Personal Digital Assistant (PDA). Also, the student may have attention problems that can result in copying errors when the schedule is found only on a board at the front of the room.

Prepare for Changes and Transitions

Teachers of students with AS will need to take care to prepare students for routine and unscheduled transitions. Visually posted or individualized schedules should highlight the expected transitions between classes and during periods such as lunch and physical education. Teachers can prepare students for transition by providing them with a laminated schedule and making changes in water soluble markers. Alternatively, sticky notes with unexpected changes can be placed upon the schedule. Teachers should take care to explain to and prepare students for any changes by not only talking about them, but, if possible, visiting the scene of the change with the student in advance. Students may need to engage in calming activities or utilize rituals to help them deal with transitions. Students can gain skills in handling unexpected transitions by learning to deal with scheduled surprises. The teacher can write the surprise into the daily schedule so that students gain experience in dealing with the unexpected. Students can be taught to identify novel situations and to then resort to a rehearsed list of steps to be taken to deal with this novelty (Klin et al., 2000).

Provide Structure for Unstructured Time

Unstructured times, such as the time before and after school, the time between classes, lunchtime, recess, using the restroom, waiting for the bus, and riding the bus, can be the most difficult parts of the day for students with AS. Teachers and other school staff must find ways to bring structure to these times. Students may need to practice the rules of these situations and have these rules available for their reference. Students may practice appropriate behavior through the use of social stories or specific scripts for the different situations.

Students may be given alternatives such as leaving for the class change early or late, and eating lunch, participating in recess, or waiting for school to begin or be dismissed in a different location than their peers. Students may benefit from having an individual "peer buddy" or group of peers (circle of friends) to support them, which also gives them the benefit of an opportunity to practice their social skills. Teachers can bring structure to unstructured times by assigning activities for the unstructured periods. The unstructured time may provide an excellent opportunity for students to work in their own area of interest. When this is not possible or practical, this could be a time that the student is earning future work time in her area of interest by demonstrating appropriate behavior.

One of the most stressful changes for the student with AS may be the times a substitute teacher takes the place of the regular teacher. Having a substitute teacher requires proactive planning on the part of the regular teacher. For some students, having a substitute may necessitate having a plan in place for instruction to take place with another, more familiar staff member.

Provide Instruction About the Hidden Curriculum

Brenda Smith Myles and Diane Adreon (2001) discuss the importance of "the set of rules that everyone in the school knows, but that no one has been directly taught," or what they call the *hidden curriculum* (pp. 97–98). This hidden curriculum must be explicitly taught to the student with AS, particularly to the student who has to deal with multiple teachers. Students need to be taught the following:

- How to tell when the teacher is happy with the student's performance.
- What the teacher does to communicate that he or she is angry.
- Which teachers the student can joke with and under what circumstances.
- What tasks are most important to the teacher (such as tests versus assignments).
- What upsets the teacher and what the teacher's pet peeves are.
- What the rules are for talking in class.
- How to ask questions during a lecture or lesson.
- Who to see if they have a problem.
- How to request help in each class.
- When and how to turn in homework and class assignments.
- How flexible the teacher is regarding late assignments.
- If the teacher allows students to negotiate due dates.
- How assignments are to be completed.
- Where the assignments can be completed.
- Where to sit in the class so that there is easy access to the teacher.
- What to do in individual classes if he does not have the right supplies or has left his homework in his locker.
- What to be doing in each class when the bell rings.
- What the penalty is for turning in assignments late, being tardy, or missing supplies. (Myles & Adreon, 2001, pp. 97–98)

Problems With Language

Although there is no clinically significant delay in the development of the language of students with AS, there may be many issues with the subtleties of language. For example, while a majority of fourth graders would understand the teacher's comment, "This assignment will be a piece of cake for you," the student with AS may be expecting dessert as a reward for the completion of the assignment. It is important that teachers be attuned to the ways that their comment or instructions, or the comments of other students, may be misinterpreted by students with AS.

Strategies and Interventions That Work for Problems With Language

Avoid or Carefully Explain Ambiguous Language Such as Idioms, Metaphors, and Figures of Speech

It is important to realize that language subtleties may be a weak area for a student who in many other ways is very capable. Teachers will need to take care to avoid and minimize the use of ambiguous language. It is also important that teachers help students with AS improve in this area by explicitly teaching the meaning of ambiguous language and preparing them to have greater capacity when such language is used. Students can actually gain understanding of double meanings as they work on understanding idioms.

Avoid or Explain the Use of Sarcasm or Jokes With Double Meanings

Although we recommend that teachers in the classroom not use sarcasm in general, it is especially important not to use such language around students with AS, as they likely will not understand the double meaning of the language. Similarly, they are likely to have difficulty with jokes that play on words, such as puns and double entendre. Because this type of humor may be commonplace with their peers, it is very important that students with AS be taught the multiple meanings of words.

Avoid or Explain the Use of Nicknames

The use of nicknames may confuse the student with AS or it may appear to him that the person using the nickname is making fun of him by using a different name for him. Again, he may need help in understanding that multiple names can be used respectfully for the same person.

Teach Students How to Find Key Words and Concepts in Directions and Instructions

The student with AS may miss the subtleties of expression or emphasis that a teacher or other speaker may use to signal a key concept. It is very helpful for these students to have the visual reminder of having a key concept written on the board or on an overhead projector. Teachers can also give students an auditory reminder to listen for certain key words. In terms of listening for key words that a teacher may use repeatedly when giving important instructions, students with AS can be taught how to do this through the use of a social story about the importance of trigger words. The students themselves can be taught how to use their own voices to emphasize certain words through the use of modified stress, rhythm, prosody, and pitch. A speech pathologist, as part of the multidisciplinary team involved in the student's education, may play an important role in teaching students with AS how to modify their own oral presentation, which in turn can serve to make them more aware of the oral presentations of others.

Problems With Abstract Reasoning

Teachers need to understand that students with AS may demonstrate strong skills, such as an ability to memorize, which may lead to advanced spelling, decoding, and reading vocabulary. This memorization also may aide students in having a strong base of factual knowledge. However, this recall of information should not mask the fact that these students may have difficulty with advanced comprehension. Teachers also may see that students with AS have problems moving from the parts to the whole and making generalizations. This difficulty with abstract reasoning may be particularly true if emotional nuances or multiple meanings are being considered.

Strategies or Interventions That Work to Improve Abstract Reasoning

Break Down the Goal of the Lesson Into Its Component Parts and Provide Supports

After completing a task analysis of the vocabulary, understanding, and skills needed for the goal of the lesson to be mastered, the instruction should be broken down into smaller units. New vocabulary must be explicitly taught. Skills that will be required to complete the lesson should be reviewed and/or taught, if they are new to the student. Finally, the key idea should be broken down into concepts that build on one another with the result of integrating the knowledge of the lessons.

Utilize "Naturalistic" Instruction

A May 2002 *TIME* Magazine article featured an extensive examination of issues related to autism. As the article reported in a review of the literature regarding education, although autistic children may respond to being taught basic knowledge through association and operant conditioning principles, students with AS need naturalistic or incidental instruction in order to establish generalizations and higher level comprehension (Nash, 2002). Naturalistic instruction places an emphasis on accepting partial responses that are spontaneous, even if they are less complete; evaluating for understanding of key concepts, actions, and vocabulary; asking open-ended questions; and encouraging higher order thinking and applications of concepts through questioning.

Provide Appropriate Accommodations Throughout Instruction

Teachers need to build into their lessons the types of supports students with AS need. These supports may include a repetition of the small units of instruction, all levels and types of prompts, pre-teaching of new concepts or vocabulary prior to group instruction, a reduced field of choice, tangible reinforcements, and peer and teacher modeling, as well as guided practice and re-teaching. Accommodations should be individualized and gradually faded as the student demonstrates the ability to learn without them.

Provide Adaptations to the Way the Lesson Will Be Taught

In order to capitalize on a student's strengths and to minimize the impact of her weaknesses, teachers will want to adapt both the way the information is presented and the way that she is asked to demonstrate her understanding. Because some students with AS have visual strengths, videos, plays, CD-ROMs, diagrams, and graphs all may serve as effective ways to present information. Similarly, students may benefit from having visual organizers on which to record key points and make abstract connections. Hands-on learning will provide a greater likelihood that students will gain an understanding of the concept, as will the use of visual, spatial, or musical patterns that offer emphasis to the spoken or written word.

Provide Explicit Instruction to Ensure Understanding of the Concept Being Taught

Teachers should not assume that students with AS understand the goal of the lesson. It is important that teachers explicitly state the concept that is being taught and the importance of each learning activity. Students with AS may miss the big picture. As the saying goes, they are concerned with the trees and not the forest.

Move From Specifics to Generalizations

Students with AS may do best with inductive reasoning, moving from the parts of a concept to the whole. Teachers should begin with specifics and gradually move to generalizations. A unifying theme will help the student to find the commonality in the pieces of information they are learning. Teachers cannot assume that AS students will make this intellectual leap without explicitly seeing connections between the pieces and the whole puzzle.

Provide Alternative Ways for Students to Demonstrate Understanding That Allow Them to Utilize Their Strengths

Teachers will have the most success with students with a variety of learning challenges, including AS, when they realize that there are different, yet equally acceptable ways for students to demonstrate understanding. Students with visual strengths may do best to demonstrate their understanding with a visual modality such as a project, diagram, or slideshow presentation. Students with auditory strengths may do best to

Teachers will have the most success with students with a variety of learning challenges, including AS, when they realize that there are different, yet equally acceptable ways for students to demonstrate understanding.

present the information orally. When testing AS students' acquisition of new knowledge, it may be helpful to have students do brief oral or written summaries of what they have learned after an activity is completed. It may be best to break down test questions so that they elicit one piece of specific information. Finally, it is important to be open to alternative strategies that the individual student may develop. Teachers should examine whether the student is using an alternative strategy and aide him or her in developing that strategy.

The following list of instructional strategies for enhancing practical comprehension can serve as a guide to teachers as they work with students with AS.

- Direct the student to the significant main ideas to be sought in reading passages by allowing him to take notes using highlighter markers or similar methods.
- Maintain a level of challenge consistent with the student's cognitive functioning level.
- Have the student practice listening for key facts and check frequently to assure that the student can repeat the main ideas once they have been identified in class discussion.
- Have the student practice inferential thinking incrementally, using one logical step at a time.
- Have the student practice judging the relevancy of information through the use of embedded distracters.
- Ask the student to predict what may happen next in a story sequence.
- Ask the student to recall sequences of detail in a story or visual presentation.
- Ask the student to identify self-contradictions in material.
- Help the student to find similarities through classification of items.

- Have the student practice practical judgment for decision making in commonplace life situations (i.e., "What would you do if _______ happened?").
- Ask the student to identify the supporting details in an identified key concept.
- Ask the student to arrange or rearrange events from a story in sequential order.
- Ask the student to differentiate fact from opinion.
- Teach the student to locate information using a table, index, dictionary, or online search.

Problems With Sensory Hyper- and Hyposensitivity

Teachers will notice that students with AS may become anxious and/or withdrawn, seemingly without reason. It will be important for the teacher and other support staff to explore the student's environment to see what may be causing discomfort for him or her and to consider what can be done to either remove the cause of the discomfort or minimize its effect. Problems in the student's environment may include sights, sounds, and smells, along with touch and taste issues. This is an area where teachers will especially want to consider whether this is a time for accommodations or a time to help the student deal with the environment as it is. Providing accommodations may be necessary if the problem is severe or if the teacher does not have time to fully prepare the student for the environmental discomfort. On the other hand, as previously discussed, if we can give the student the tools to handle this hypersensitivity, we can help him to become more independent over time. Care should also be given to balance the student's real needs for accommodations with the fact that providing the accommodation may unintentionally reinforce the hypersensitivity and may also serve to make the child stand out more from his peers.

Strategies or Interventions That Work to Deal With Hyper- and Hyposensitivity

Alter or Change the Environment to Decrease Factors to Which the Student may be Hyper- or Hyposensitive

The teacher, with the help of staff such as the occupational therapist, should analyze the environment to see what factors may be impacting the individual student with AS. When possible, the environment can be changed. For example, a student can be seated away from humming lights, fans, or bright sunlight. An area with strong odor can be ventilated. In extreme cases, students with AS may wear gloves to avoid an unpleasant touch or work with a partner who will handle any difficult materials. For irritating sounds, the teacher may be able to minimize the noise. If not, the students could be provided with earplugs or allowed to listen to their own music to camouflage the noise.

Work Proactively to Prepare the Student to Deal With His Issues Around Hyper- and Hyposensitivity

Teachers should preview with students situations such as fire drills or science experiments that they know will be coming up that may impact the student's hyper- or hyposensitivity. A social story is a good way to provide this preview. Teachers should look for behavioral indicators that the student may be beginning to experience sensitivities. Students with AS should be encouraged to report their own sensitivities or pain. Teachers should help students to learn to advocate for and use their own accommodations to help with their sensitivities.

Employ Strategies That Serve to Help the Students to Calm Themselves

Many students benefit from an alternative place to go in the class to calm themselves. A beanbag or rocking chair may serve this purpose. Sensory integration activities such as compression, massage, vibration, brushing, "brain gym," heavy movement, rhythmic sustained movement (trampoline, bouncing a ball, marching), chewing gum, chewing on a toy, or using a water bottle may provide a student with AS with the needed break or relief when he or she is experiencing sensory hypersensitivity. Some of the things on this list may be familiar and easily accessible to the classroom teacher while others will certainly require consultation with an occupational therapist or expert in autism spectrum disorders. (See additional strategies in the next section on problems dealing with the regulation of anxiety, depression, and emotions.)

Problems With Anxiety, Depression, and Emotional Regulation

It is not hard to imagine that students who are bright and who are able to see that they are having trouble with both the academic and social demands of the school environment would experience difficulties with their emotional regulation. Teachers may notice signs of anxiety and depression as students anticipate, attempt to cope with, and then react to their problems in the classroom and school. Although the American Psychiatric Association's *DSM-IV* does not specifically list emotional issues as an indicator of AS, these issues have been discussed in previous chapters and are often present in students with AS. Ideally, staff will incorporate other strategies that we have previously mentioned in a proactive way, so that students do not become emotionally upset. Despite the best efforts of parents and teachers, students will become anxious or depressed at times. It is then crucial that parents and teachers observe and identify the signs of distress early and intervene.

Strategies or Interventions That Work With Anxiety, Depression, and Emotional Regulation

Work to Proactively Minimize Situations That Will Cause Emotional Problems

School staff should work together with parents to identify triggers for behavioral problems. An informal or formal Functional Behavioral Analysis (FBA) can be designed to take a systematic look at the antecedents of the behavior, the behavior itself, and the consequences that typically follow. After a detailed analysis of the current behavior, a Behavior Intervention Plan (BIP) can be devised to help to structure the environment in a way that promotes individual student success. For individual students, their day may need to be structured so that they avoid crowded or noisy places. Alternatively, some students may need to leave crowded or noisy places early before they become overly anxious. Students can be given permission to move through halls early or late if these situations produce anxiety.

Although behavior problems are not unusual at home and at school, they are not always a major presenting problem in AS. Negative behavioral outbursts are most frequently related to frustration, being thwarted, or difficulties in compliance when a particularly rigid response pattern has been challenged or interrupted. Rebecca Moyes (2002), a parent of a child with AS, has presented a viewpoint on the development of behavior management plans for children with AS. She stresses the importance of first attempting to analyze the communicative intent of the negative behavior. She devalues the effectiveness of punishment and suggests a hierarchy of negative consequences when necessary, emphasizing the value of positive behavioral incentives.

Identify Signs of Stress and/or Overstimulation Early and Intervene Before the Problem Becomes Overwhelming

School staff should be aware of particular signs that show that an individual student is becoming anxious or depressed. These signs may include behaviors such as covering or plugging ears, squeezing body parts, or an increase in repetitive behaviors such as rocking or picking at their skin.

Allow and Encourage Students to Employ Techniques That Will Allow for Self-Calming and Regaining Emotional Control

Some typical strategies that can be put into place include providing periodic breaks; providing students with a checklist of steps for self-calming; providing a visual signal to students to use their calming techniques; teaching students how to ask for help, sometimes using an agreed-upon signal; using sensory techniques such as those discussed in the previous section on dealing with hypersensitivity; allowing the student to listen to calming music; allowing students to refer to words that help them to calm down; and allowing students do a favorite activity. Other calming techniques the student can employ on his own include relaxation, deep breathing, guided visualization, or meditation.

Allow Students to Move to a Special Area in the Classroom or Building

Student may also need to move to a special area in the room or building, for a quiet time out, to utilize sensory integration equipment, and/or to interact with specially trained staff. Depending on the program, this area may be within the classroom or in another part of the school building. If the student is moving to another part of the school building, it is crucial that there be a special educator, counselor, or psychologist there to help the student work through his issues.

Help Students to Gain Skills in Monitoring and Responding to Their Own Behavior

Students may use a visual system such as a behavioral chart or "stress thermometer" to monitor where they are in terms of level of stress or discomfort. Students can also give themselves scores on a behavioral contract and earn extra points when their scores match up with the staff member's view of how they are doing.

Teach Students to Prepare for Stressful, Overstimulating, and Uncomfortable Situations

Students can preview difficult situations by using social stories (Gray & White, 2002). A social skills lesson can also preview difficult situations and provide students an opportunity to discuss and roleplay how they will handle it. For example, a community outing, such as a field trip, can be rehearsed ahead of time. The mode of transportation and route can be researched before the trip. Anticipated interactions can be scripted and practiced. The components of potentially stressful situations can be generalized into rules that can be practiced and learned.

Consider Medication With a Psychiatrist or Pediatrician and Behavioral Consultation With a Psychologist or Behavior Specialist

When behaviors are continuing to interfere with education, despite the efforts of staff to provide adaptations, accommodations, and instruction designed to improve the situation, parents should be open to seeking out the advice of experts outside of the school building who may recommend other behavioral or medical interventions. Currently, there are no reliable guidelines for the application of medications specifically for AS. However, many of the symptoms and coexisting conditions are treated, in some cases, with medication. For example, attention problems, impulsivity, anxiety, depression, and illogical thought patterns are all being addressed with medication with some measure of success in individual cases.

Problems With Attention, Organization, and Other Areas of Executive Functioning

It is important for teachers to realize that although students with AS may be very focused and organized when it come to their areas of passion, they are likely to have problems with attention and organization that affect their work production in school.

It is important for teachers to realize that although students with AS may be very focused and organized when it come to their areas of passion, they are likely to have problems with attention and organization that affect their work production in school. Students with AS may have problems with any and all areas of executive functioning. Dr. Martha Denckla (1994) identified the major areas of executive functioning as initiating, sustaining, inhibiting, and shifting. In simple terms, initiating means beginning a task, sustaining refers to staying on task and completion of tasks, inhibiting refers to blocking out other distracting thoughts or actions that are not directly related to the task, and shifting means moving from one part of the task to another or leaving one task entirely to move to another. The core issues of AS that we have described above, particularly the student's problems with social interactions and with very focused areas of interest and expertise, may impact all of these executive functioning areas. Problems with language, abstract reasoning, anxiety, and need for predictability all impact executive functioning, as well. All of the strategies that previously have been mentioned will have a positive impact on the student's focus and organization. There also are some interventions that are particularly targeted toward increasing executive functioning skills that will be effective in helping students with AS be more attentive and productive in the classroom.

Strategies or Interventions That Work to Deal With Attention, Organization, and Other Areas of Executive Functioning

Use Visual Schedules

As previously discussed, students with AS often will respond better to a visual schedule that provides for predictability, utilizes their strengths, and aids them in being more attentive and organized. The visual schedule may be displayed for the entire group, but also can be individualized for the student. It may be arranged vertically or horizontally and display activities by using words and/or graphics or icons in a variety of colors and font sizes. Velcro or laminated strips could allow the students to remove the item from the schedule when it is completed.

Use Proximity to and Prompting From the Teacher

Many students with AS will work best if seated close to the teacher, so that they can be frequently cued, redirected, prompted, and rewarded for success. A signal from the teacher, whether it is a word or gesture, may help keep the student with AS focused. It is crucial for the teacher to first make sure he or she has engaged the student. It is only then that he or she can work on helping the student to understand the concept. To ensure engagement, it is crucial that the student has completed his previous activity. For the student with AS, completing activities previously assigned may require waiting for a break, a completion of the activity before this one, or getting compliance to complete the activity by receiving a warning that time is almost up (Shapiro, 2006).

Structure Work Periods

Students with AS may benefit from having work periods broken down into smaller segments and having a clear definition of what they are expected to accomplish during that work period. A timer or stopwatch can bring even more definition to the time period. Some students with AS will need an adjusted workload for class or homework assignments. It is helpful for teachers to visually indicate where on the page the student is to stop, such as drawing a line after the last problem or question the student is to complete.

Structure the Environment

Students with AS may be able to focus better when their auditory and visual distractions are limited. Some students work best when provided with a study carrel or "office" in which to complete their work. They may need the boundaries of their personal space clearly defined, even to the extent of having colored tape on the floor to mark off the area. Other students with AS may respond to the use of an FM system that allows them to listen to the teacher over headphones as the teacher's voice is transmitted electronically via a microphone. The potential negative impact of both of these suggestions is that they may separate and make the student appear even more different than the other students in the classroom if he or she is the only student provided with this type of accommodation. However, for some students with AS, this difference would allow them to stand out less than their inattentive, nonproductive behavior may be already making them appear to others.

Teach Students to Monitor Their Own Attention

As we strive to move students from dependence to independence, it is crucial that we provide them with tools that allow them to monitor their own level of attention, energy, and arousal. Many occupational therapists have expertise with programs like ALERT (Williams & Shellenberger, 1996), which aims to teach students to monitor "how their engine is running" and to self-regulate by making appropriate adjustments.

Utilize Visual Supports That Aide With Completion of Assignments

Again, teachers should utilize the visual strengths of students with AS to support them in areas that may be weaker, such as organization. Teacher should post visual reminders of the organizational steps needed to complete a variety of assignments. Within an individual assignment, teachers can highlight directions and steps. Color-coding of directions can be an effective tool. Teachers should visually model the steps that are needed for completion of the project or assignment, as well as provide a model of what the end product will look like.

Support Organization With Rubrics, Study Guides, and Outlines

Students with AS and their parents and/or tutors who are supporting them in completing their assignments at home will benefit from receiving a clear rubric that tells what is expected in the assignment, when each part of the assignment should be completed, and what criteria will be used for evaluating the assignment. Students can then gain experience in monitoring their own progress on assignments and in evaluating how well they have met the expectations of the assignment. Outlines and study guides that specify what material is to be covered and where students can go to find additional information are very helpful to students as they attempt to learn course content. Providing written summaries of key concepts or a reminder of where to find those in the text may be crucial for students with AS who may have difficulty with conceptually organizing what they have been taught. Teachers can use the Bordering on Excellence Organization tool (see Figure 1), to analyze what organizational demands may be present in their planned lesson. They will make notes of the organizational obstacles in the middle of the frame and then quickly circle the interventions listed around the sides of the frame that can remove those obstacles and provide access to instruction for students with AS (Weinfeld et al., 2006).

Provide Classroom Structures That Support Organization of Materials

Many students with AS will benefit from having clearly designated areas for materials within the classroom. This includes having clearly labeled areas in which to put their own materials, as well as places to put work that still needs to be completed and finished assignments. A color-coded binder or pocket folder system can help a student to organize multiple subject areas or classes.

Utilize Technology

Fortunately, there are increasingly technological solutions available to aide students with organization. Electronic organizers are commonplace in the adult world and can provide support to students with AS in organizing their tasks and commitments. A study by Ferguson, Myles, and Hagiwara (2005) showed that Personal Digital Assistants (PDA) were effective in decreasing students with disabilities' reliance on adults to complete tasks at home and at school. Laptop computers and even the less-expensive portable keyboards, such as Alphasmart, Dana, or Neo, have Palm Pilot capability. Software organizational programs, such as Inspiration, help students who are visual thinkers to web their ideas and turn them into an outline with the click of a keystroke. And, we can count on the fact that technology will continue to become more accessible, offer more options, and become easier to use. Students in our schools are becoming increasingly experienced and intuitive in the use of ever-expanding technology.

Adaptations/Accommodations

ORGANIZATION

Possible Stumbling Blocks

- following multistep directions
- planning the steps needed to complete a task
- organizing desk, locker, notebook, and other materials
- locating needed materials
- breaking long-range assignments into manageable steps
- prioritizing

Instructional Materials

- visual models, storyboards, Venn diagrams, matrices, and flow charts
- study guides that assist with locating information and answers
- highlighters, index tabs, and colored stickers
- assignment books and calendars for recording assignments
- outlines, webs, diagrams, and other graphic organizers

NOTES:

Teaching/Assessment Methods

- use short, simple directions
- post class and homework assignments in the same area each day and assure that students record them and/or have a printed copy
- verbally review class and homework assignments
- work with students to establish specific due dates for short assignments and time frames for long-term assignments
- break up tasks into workable and obtainable steps
- provide checkpoints for long-term assignments and monitor progress frequently
- provide homework hotline or structured homework assistance
- provide a specific location for students to place completed work

Assistive Technology

- electronic organizers
- software organization programs
- audiotaping assignments
- e-mailing assignments from school to student's home account

Figure 1. Bordering on Excellence Organization Tool

Note. From *Smart Kids With Learning Difficulties: Overcoming Obstacles and Realizing Potential* (p. 118), by R. Weinfeld, L. Barnes-Robinson, S. Jeweler, and B. Roffman-Shevitz, 2006, Waco, TX: Prufrock Press. Copyright ©2006 Prufrock Press. Reprinted with permission.

Provide Systematic Supports for Organizational Help

Many schools routinely provide organizational support for all students. Providing a structured time and way for all students to record their assignments, including the use of an assignment book, can be extremely helpful for students with AS. Students with AS may need the added support of the teacher actually checking to see that they have recorded the assignment accurately. There also needs to be back-up systems in place, so that the parents of students with AS and the students themselves can clarify what their assignments are after they have left the classroom. Some excellent back-up systems include the use of technology—more and more teachers are now posting their assignments and grades online so students and their parents can access them at any time. This has huge benefits for supporting the organization of students with AS. E-mail also allows parents or students to quickly communicate with teachers to clarify assignments. Some schools even post assignments on a voicemail system, often called a homework hotline. Finally, students with AS can benefit from having the contact information for other students who they can call on for clarification of assignments. Many students are already using instant messaging (IM) for this purpose.

Structure Time During the School Day for Organization of Assignments and Materials

Students with AS will benefit from a daily time during the school day to learn organizational skills and have a chance to apply them to their current demands. This time may happen during the regular course of instruction or it may be a pull-out period or resource class where the student with AS meets with a special educator who helps him to review what needs to be done, how will it be done, and when will it be done.

Problems With Motor Issues, Including Written Production

Teachers will notice that many students with AS have either fine and/or gross motor issues. These issues may interfere with a variety of physical requirements of the school day including physical education and recess, other activities that involve movement, and self-care. In terms of the academic expectations of the classroom, motor issues may especially impact students when they are required to perform written tasks, whether those are the writing of words or numbers. Teachers may want to seek out the expertise of related service providers, such as physical therapists or occupational therapists, who can provide specific instruction to the student and strategies that the teachers may employ to improve the student's ability to access typical learning activities throughout the school day. It is important to keep in mind that we are preparing students for a world that relies more and more upon the use of technology. Although we offer some solutions for helping students with their handwriting below, we believe that emphasis should be placed on having students with handwriting problems gain expertise with the technology that will allow them to communicate their ideas without being held back by their motor issues.

Strategies and Interventions That Work to Deal With Motor Issues Including Written Production

Provide Support With and Alternatives to Physical Education and Recess

Physical education and recess may be challenging times for students with AS, both because of their problems with fine and gross motor skills and because of other issues, especially their social issues. Competitive sports may be particularly difficult for students with AS. Kids with AS may need these periods of the day adapted in ways that ensure they are being asked to do activities in which they can be successful. Some students with AS may need a separate period of physical education instruction that focuses on developing the skills that they are lacking.

Although schools don't typically think of providing support with recess, without any support this may be the worst time of the day for a student with AS who may need an adult to help structure activities and make sure the level of physical demand is appropriate. If this support is not possible, it may be necessary to provide an alternative, safe place for the student with AS to go during recess.

Support in Acquiring Written Language Skills

Students with AS may need very targeted and specific instruction in order to improve their handwriting ability. This instruction may include specific directions about how to hold writing implements and the paper, as well as instruction in the formation of the letters. A structured, supportive handwriting approach, such as Handwriting Without Tears, created by Jan Olsen, can help provide this instruction. Handwriting Without Tears is a developmental program that offers basic exercises in figure-ground discrimination and top-to-bottom and left-to-right sequencing.

Provide Tools That Allow for Improvement of Handwriting

Students may benefit from a variety of tools that ease problems related to handwriting. Some helpful tools include special paper with raised lines, pencil grips, mechanical pencils for students who press too hard, markers that require minimal pressure for students who press too lightly, and the use of graph paper or vertically lined paper to help with written organization in math. An occupational therapist can help with access to these materials, as well as offer additional suggestions.

Provide Alternatives That Allow Students to Write More Easily or Circumvent Writing

First and foremost, teachers need to analyze whether or not writing is really the goal of the lesson. There will be times when a written activity is the actual goal, but in many other cases, writing is only one of many ways to learn and demonstrate understanding. When writing is not the goal of the lesson, students with AS should be allowed and encouraged to demonstrate understanding in alternative ways, such as creating a diagram, graph, or model, or drawing scenes (storyboarding). When note taking is required, students may be provide with a set of the teacher's notes or another student may be asked to use NCR (no carbon required) paper, which automatically produces a second set of notes that can be given to the student with AS. Teachers may find the Bordering on Excellence Writing tool (see Figure 2) an effective way to analyze their lessons and see what obstacles involving written language may be inherent in their planned instruction. After analyzing the lesson and making notes of the obstacles in the middle of the "border," teachers can then quickly circle the interventions that will remove the obstacles and allow the student with AS access to the instruction.

When writing is not the goal of the lesson, students with AS should be allowed and encouraged to demonstrate understanding in alternative ways . . .

Allow and Encourage Students to Use Technology as an Alternative to Handwriting

Ever-improving assistive technology programs in schools provide students with many alternatives for expressing their ideas and demonstrating their understanding. Students with AS

Adaptations/Accommodations

WRITING

Possible Stumbling Blocks

- the physical act of putting words on paper
- handwriting
- generating topics
- formulating topic sentences
- combining words into meaningful sentences
- using language mechanics effectively (e.g., grammar, punctuation, spelling)
- organizing sentences and incorporating adequate details and support statements into organized paragraphs
- revising and editing

Instructional Materials

- step-by-step written directions
- a proofreading checklist
- scoring rubrics, models, and anchor papers for students to evaluate their own work
- graphic organizers
- guides such as story starters, webs, story charts, outlines
- dictionaries, word banks, and thesauri
- personal dictionaries of misused and misspelled words
- highlighter to indicate errors/corrections
- copy of teacher notes or of another student's notes (NCR paper)
- pencil grips
- paper with raised lines
- mechanical pencils
- slant board

NOTES:

Teaching/Assessment Methods

- focus on content rather than mechanics
- focus on quality rather than quantity
- begin with storyboards, guided imagery, dramatization, or projects before the writing process
- set important purposes for writing, such as writing for publication, writing to an expert, or writing to a famous person
- allow students to write in area of interest or expertise
- allow students to demonstrate understanding through alternative methods/products
- reduce or alter written requirements
- break down assignments into smaller, manageable parts
- additional time
- work with partners or small groups to confer for revising, editing, and proofreading

Assistive Technology

- voice recognition software
- organizational software
- electronic spellers and dictionaries
- tape recorder for student dictation and then transcription
- computer word processor with spelling and grammar checker or talking word processor
- portable keyboards
- word prediction software
- programs that allow writing to be read aloud
- programs that provide for audio spell checker, word prediction, and homophone distinction

Figure 2. Bordering on Excellence Writing Tool

Note. From *Smart Kids With Learning Difficulties: Overcoming Obstacles and Realizing Potential* (p. 116), by R. Weinfeld, L. Barnes-Robinson, S. Jeweler, and B. Roffman-Shevitz, 2006, Waco, TX: Prufrock Press. Copyright ©2006 Prufrock Press. Reprinted with permission.

can work on a word processor or portable keyboard, many of which have built on programs for checking spelling and grammar. Software programs, such as Co-Writer, allow a student to type the first letters of a word and then see choices of the word she may be trying to write. Write Out Loud allows the student's writing to be read to her so she can see if in fact she has written what she intended. Inspiration and Draft Builder allow students to move from ideas to written compositions. PowerPoint allows students to create a presentation of their ideas, focusing on their visual skills.

Problems With Ritualistic, Repetitive, or Rigid Behavior

Teachers may observe that some students with AS have routines or rituals that they do repetitively. This may include hand or finger flapping or twisting, complex whole-body movements, or the persistent preoccupation with objects or parts of objects. Teachers will need to work with parents and other professionals to determine when and if to allow the behavior and how to minimize the impact of the behavior on social interactions and academic performance. It is important to realize that most of this behavior is not willful and should not be responded to as if the student was intentionally doing something bad or disobedient. At the Harbour Schools of Annapolis and Baltimore, whenever possible, students are taught to modify their ritualistic or repetitive movement into something that's less noticeable and fits in more with the neurotypical world.

Strategies and Interventions That Work to Deal With Ritualistic, Repetitive, or Rigid Behavior

Develop a Functional Behavioral Analysis (FBA)

School personnel can develop an FBA with input from the parents. The FBA should accurately describe the behavior, analyze the antecedents to that behavior, and describe the current consequences and rewards to see whether they are in fact helping to extinguish the behavior or reinforcing it. It is also crucial to look at the purposes of the behavior and to determine if there is a replacement behavior that can be developed. Part of the Behavior Intervention Plan (BIP) that is devised after the FBA is completed may be a determination that the current, undesirable behavior will be allowed at certain times of the day or week.

If Possible, Intervene Before the Behavior Becomes a Habit, Distracting, or Disruptive

Teachers may use a variety of strategies to proactively work on the behavior. Counselors, psychologists, and special educators are all valuable resources for helping to work on behavior. Students can be helped to rehearse appropriate behavior. Social stories dealing with examples of appropriate behavior can help students to prepare for positive behavior. Once again, using students' visual strengths by providing them with written directions and visual reminders of appropriate behaviors are helpful strategies for students with AS.

Respond to Behaviors in a Way That Will Help Minimize the Impact of the Behavior and/or Extinguish It

Teachers who work with students with AS will need to develop a carefully thought-out plan that focuses on when to ignore the behavior, when to distract the student and try to introduce a new activity, when to reward the student for refraining from the behavior, and when to enforce consequences on the student for displaying the behavior.

Conclusion

Teachers can make school a successful experience for students with AS when they work proactively in conjunction with parents and other professionals to put strategies in place that will address the issues of these students and increase their possibilities of reaching their true potential.

Students with AS demonstrate a variety of school problems and behaviors that may make it difficult for them to be successful in the classroom. Teachers can be of great help to these students when they recognize that these problems and behaviors are part of the student's unique profile. Even more importantly, teachers can make school a successful experience for students with AS when they work proactively in conjunction with parents and other professionals to put strategies in place that will address the issues of these students and increase their possibilities of reaching their true potential.

In the next chapter, we will discuss the range of school options that might appropriately serve students with AS and look at how parents can effectively access these services and programs.

chapter 7

Working With the School System: Options for Students With AS

AS we enter the Asperger's program of the Ivymount School in Potomac, MD, the students have been participating in a cooperative game that requires listening to one another and taking turns. The activity is led by the school's psychologist and speech pathologist and is part of a regularly scheduled time that is devoted to developing social skills every day. The teacher and two instructional assistants also are present in the room. John has become very agitated, because he feels that he did not get a chance to do what he wanted in the game. In return, Sam has become irritated with John's behavior. The other four 5th and 6th graders also seem agitated, as we hear more audible groans and two of the students begin flapping their hands. The adults direct the students to return to their seats. Everyone goes back to their desk and the speech pathologist begins to lead a discussion about two good things that happened during the group time and two problematic things that happened.

On each student's desk is an individual daily schedule with a behavioral chart incorporated into it. There is also a large visual schedule in the front of the room. Students are carefully prepared for any changes in the schedule. Both the student and teacher rates each of the behaviors listed on the student's individual contract. If the student's assessment of his or her behavior matches that of the teacher, he or she will get extra match points. Points are turned in for rewards. Each student also has two individual goal areas and a self-monitoring chart on his or her desk. It is color coded from green, meaning "smooth ride;" to yellow, meaning "experiencing some turbulence;" to red, meaning "meteor shower." Velcro holds the star that indicates where the student is on scale with each behavior during the class. If the student is moving to yellow or red on his chart, then he is expected to use his individualized strategies to move back to green.

The students talk about how they might handle things differently in the next group time, referring to the visual strategies "to get you back on green" that are posted on the board. They also refer to the posted list of things that they can do to help another student that is having problems. Sam is still very upset and calling out, and as a result, he is quietly directed to go to the time-out room with the psychologist to have some quiet, calming time and then to discuss the incident. John requests and is allowed to go to the sensory integration area, which is called the space station. He puts on a body sock, referred to as the space suit, to help him calm down. After about 4 minutes, he returns to the group, appearing to be very much under control. As the discussion ends, students are given some down time before the next activity—a social studies lesson involving a written language assignment—will begin. During this down time, one student relaxes on a comfortable chair, two students play games on their laptops, and one searches for information on the Internet.

The class moves into social studies. They are talking about writing historical fiction to tell a story that has to do with the period of history that they have been studying. This is a way of relating an area of interest (in this case, the Lascaux caves in France) to having them write a story, a skill that is a weak area for all of them. The teacher has the tasks of the writing assignment broken down per day, so that the students know what part of the assignment they have to complete each day in order to finish by the end of the week. Everything is spelled out very thoroughly. One of the students is very resistant to writing the historical fiction and is groaning loudly. He is able to tell the teacher that he doesn't want to do it. The teacher tells him if he comes in tomorrow with another proposal, she will listen to it.

It's now time to begin preparing to go home. Toby is upset when he looks at the schedule of the day and sees that they didn't do one of their scheduled activities. The teacher explains that she was out of the room for a while unexpectedly today and they didn't get to it. She summarizes that sometimes things happen and we have to be flexible. That seems OK with Toby, but the teacher has another child to deal with. Sam is upset that he has a lot of points saved up from good behavior on his contract, and he wants to buy things now, but the teacher reminds him that they buy things at lunchtime. She calmly repeats that the rule is that they can only buy things at lunchtime. She takes the time patiently to go over the rules again. He continues to insist that he wants to buy something now and that he didn't get the opportunity to do so at lunchtime. The teacher helps him understand what he might do next time, if he sees that he's not getting a chance to buy his reward during lunch. After listening calmly to him, she is able to redirect Sam to go back to his desk to pack up to go home.

Ivymount's Asperger's program is an example of one exemplary program that provides services for students with AS. Students in this program require the intensive and integrated services that are provided by Ivymount's expert staff. Their needs cannot be adequately met in their neighborhood public schools and they must travel, in some cases long distances, and be separated from their neurotypical peers, to take part in a program that meets their needs. Like students with other disabilities, each case of a student with AS must be evaluated individually in order for a determination to be made of what the least restrictive educational environment for that student should be. Each school district should have a continuum of services, ranging from educating students in their neighborhood school with appropriate special education instruction and accommodations available in the regular classroom; to special classes for all or part of the day in a neighborhood school; to a special program located in a public school in the district, other than the neighborhood school; to a special program, in a separate building, serving only students with disabilities, such as Ivymount.

When a parent or teacher suspects that a student has a disability such as AS that is impacting her educational progress, they have a responsibility to ask that a school meeting be convened to discuss the student and to plan for appropriate interventions.

When a parent or teacher suspects that a student has a disability such as AS that is impacting her educational progress, they have a responsibility to ask that a school meeting be convened to discuss the student and to plan for appropriate interventions. These meetings will generally begin in the form of a parent-teacher conference and then move to a schoolwide child study team and finally to a 504 or IEP meeting if typical school interventions are not enough to make a difference for the student.

The Road Map in Figure 3 gives parents and teachers a visual map of the path they should follow to get appropriate services

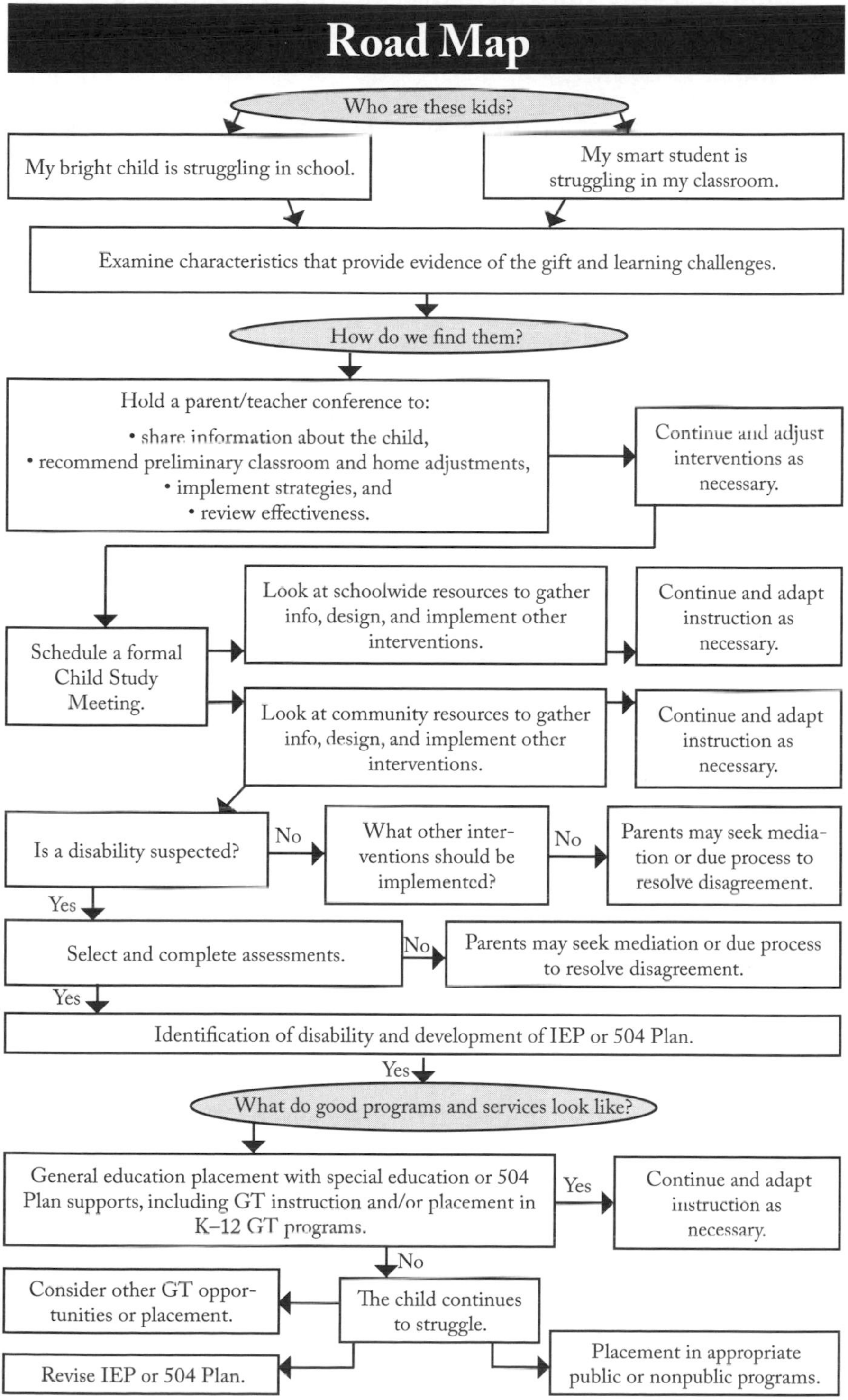

Road Map

Who are these kids?

- My bright child is struggling in school.
- My smart student is struggling in my classroom.

Examine characteristics that provide evidence of the gift and learning challenges.

How do we find them?

Hold a parent/teacher conference to:

- share information about the child,
- recommend preliminary classroom and home adjustments,
- implement strategies, and
- review effectiveness.

→ Continue and adjust interventions as necessary.

Schedule a formal Child Study Meeting.

→ Look at schoolwide resources to gather info, design, and implement other interventions. → Continue and adapt instruction as necessary.

→ Look at community resources to gather info, design, and implement other interventions. → Continue and adapt instruction as necessary.

Is a disability suspected?

- No → What other interventions should be implemented? → No → Parents may seek mediation or due process to resolve disagreement.
- Yes → Select and complete assessments.
  - No → Parents may seek mediation or due process to resolve disagreement.
  - Yes → Identification of disability and development of IEP or 504 Plan.

Yes →

What do good programs and services look like?

General education placement with special education or 504 Plan supports, including GT instruction and/or placement in K–12 GT programs.

- Yes → Continue and adapt instruction as necessary.
- No → The child continues to struggle.
  - Consider other GT opportunities or placement.
  - Revise IEP or 504 Plan.
  - Placement in appropriate public or nonpublic programs.

Figure 3. Road Map

Note. From *Smart Kids With Learning Difficulties: Overcoming Obstacles and Realizing Potential* (p. 8), by R. Weinfeld, L. Barnes-Robinson, S. Jeweler, and B. Roffman Shevitz, 2006, Waco, TX: Prufrock Press.

for a student who has AS and is struggling in school. For some students, the parent conference or child study team recommendations may be enough to provide the interventions that are necessary for the student with AS to be successful. For others, a formalized 504 plan will communicate to all staff the need for accommodations in the classroom and in testing situations. For still others, an IEP will be necessary to provide the direct special education instruction and/or school placement that will allow the student to achieve, while minimizing the impact of his or her disability.

Advocating for Appropriate Services

As parents and teachers advocate for appropriate service for students with AS, it will be crucial that they are aware of the laws and policies that will affect the decision making regarding those services. Below, we will describe some of the key terminology and issues, including the decision of a 504 plan versus an IEP; the definition of Least Restrictive Environment (LRE); the definition of the disability codes that are most likely to be discussed; and the definition of educational impact.

In our experience it is extremely helpful if parents and at least one school staff member are allied in their beliefs regarding the appropriate services that are needed for the student. It is especially important that parents try to reach a common understanding of what is needed with their ally on the school staff before heading into the formal 504 or IEP meeting. At times, one team member may dominate the formal meeting; therefore, it may be difficult for other parties to speak up. Knowing that there is a school staff person who shares their views often can make all the difference in parents being able to effectively communicate about what is needed for their child.

Having an outside educational consultant or attorney accompany the parents to the school meeting also can be very beneficial. This outside expert will have reviewed all of the child's records, observed the child in the school setting, and spoken informally with both parents and school staff about the student's strengths and needs. Having such a person by their side allows the parent to simply be a parent, focusing on their own feelings and beliefs that have led them to this meeting, while the expert can focus on the laws, policies, and dynamics of the decision making. The expert's combined knowledge of what should happen in the meeting and his or her knowledge of the student helps make for a persuasive case for providing the needed services. It has been our experience that the most effective advocates are those who are knowledgeable and persistent, rather that aggressive and confrontational. The overall goal should be to set a positive climate where everyone will be interested in collaborating for the student's best interest.

504 vs. IEP

Students with AS may qualify for a 504 plan or an IEP. Although these are both formal, legal documents that support students with disabilities, there are important differences between the two types of plans. When it is determined that a student has a disability such as AS, a 504 team or an IEP team can then determine whether or not the student qualifies for services under that plan. A 504 plan typically provides only for accommodations. Accommodations for a student with AS might include many of the suggestions in Chapters 5 and 6 of this book. An IEP could include many of the same accommodations, but would also include specific measurable goals that special educators would work on with the student over the coming year. Typically, an IEP provides for direct instruction by the special educator. For a student with AS, that direct instruction could be focused on helping the student to improve in any of the areas that are affected by his or her disability. For example, the student might have instruction in improving social skills, attention skills, organization skills, and/or written language skills. An IEP could result in the student being in a special class for part or all of the day, as well as the possibility that a student could be placed in a special program or school. In qualifying for an IEP, the team considers whether or not there is educational impact to the student's disability and whether or not she needs specially designed instruction to address that impact. In determining whether a student qualifies for a 504 plan, a school team looks at whether learning is affected to the point that the student cannot perform as well as the average student. School teams are often more willing to agree to a 504 plan than an IEP, because a 504 plan typically does not require the provision of staff time or resources.

Determination of a Disability for Students With AS

When a parent or teacher suspects a disability in a child, an Individualized Education Plan meeting should be requested in writing to the school administrator. The first IEP meeting, typically referred to as a Screening IEP meeting, will look at the student's educational history, a classroom observation, and a teacher report, along with a report from the parents. The IEP team, typically consisting of a school administrator, a special educator, the child's classroom teacher, the parents, and other school experts such as a school psychologist and/or a speech pathologist, together will discuss the data and attempt to reach consensus about whether or not a disability is suspected. If a disability is suspected, a plan for evaluation will be developed and a second IEP meeting will be scheduled to review the evaluation, make a determination about whether a disability exists, and determine whether an IEP should be developed for the student. The evaluation itself should include a review of any private evaluations that the parents may want to submit, as well as those that will be completed by appropriate school personnel, including the school psychologist and special educator. The timeline for holding the second IEP meeting is typically within 60 days of the date that the parents authorize that the evaluation process go forward. Students with AS typically would be considered for a disability code of autism, because AS is considered to be on the autism spectrum. However, the student could be considered for any of the 15 federal educational disability codes. Below are the definitions of the most likely codes for which a student with AS might be considered. These disability code definitions are taken from the Individuals with Disabilities Education Act (IDEA) revisions of 2006. This is the federal law that governs special education.

Coding for Autism—Code #14

The most likely, and generally the most accurate, educational disability coding for a student with AS is the code for autism. Parents may want to submit reports from a private psychologist, psychiatrist, and/or pediatrician to help the school in its determination of the presence of this disability. Although there is a difference between high-functioning autism, PDD-NOS, and AS, as discussed earlier in this book, they all would be covered by this category of disability coding. The definition from IDEA is as follows:

> (1)(i) *Autism* means a developmental disability significantly affecting verbal and nonverbal communication and social interaction, generally evident before age three, that adversely affects a child's educational performance. Other characteristics often associated with autism are engage-

ment in repetitive activities and stereotyped movements, resistance to environmental change or change in daily routines, and unusual responses to sensory experiences.

(ii) Autism does not apply if a child's educational performance is adversely affected primarily because the child has an emotional disturbance, as defined in paragraph (c)(4) of this section.

(iii) A child who manifests the characteristics of autism after age three could be identified as having autism if the criteria in paragraph (c)(1)(i) of this section are satisfied. (IDEA, 2006, p. 218)

Coding for Emotional Disturbance—Code #06

There are times that the concern that is presenting itself to the school staff is mainly behavioral. The school team, including parents, may be unaware that the student has AS or may feel that this condition is secondary to his emotional problems. We do want to caution parents and school staff that what may appear to be emotional disturbance may, in fact, be a result of the frustration, anxiety, and/or depression the student is experiencing as a result of her needs related to AS not being met. Parents and school staff should be further cautioned that placement of children with AS in a class of students with emotional disturbances may be a serious mismatch of educational and instructional goals. Emotional disturbance is defined in IDEA as follows:

What may appear to be emotional disturbance may, in fact, be a result of the frustration, anxiety, and/or depression the student is experiencing as a result of her needs related to AS not being met.

(4)(i) Emotional disturbance means a condition exhibiting one or more of the following characteristics over a long period of time and to a marked degree that adversely affects a child's educational performance:

(a) An inability to learn that cannot be explained by intellectual, sensory, or health factors.

(b) An inability to build or maintain satisfactory interpersonal relationships with peers and teachers.

(c) Inappropriate types of behavior or feelings under normal circumstances.

(d) A general pervasive mood of unhappiness or depression.

(e) A tendency to develop physical symptoms or fears associated with personal or school problems.

(ii) Emotional disturbance includes schizophrenia. The term does not apply to children who are socially maladjusted, unless it is determined that they have an emotional disturbance under paragraph (c)(4)(i) of this section. (IDEA, 2006, p. 218)

Coding for Other Health Impairment—Code #08

Students with AS may be considered for coding as students who are "other health impaired." This consideration may be appropriate, as the student's educational progress may also be affected by a health condition such as ADHD or Tourette's syndrome. However, once again, in an effort to accurately code students, it is important that effects of the AS be evaluated and understood. It may, in fact, be the case that the lack of attention or limited alertness that the student is demonstrating is more related to the mismatch between his needs and the school environment than it is to any other health condition. Other health impairment is defined in IDEA as follows:

(9) *Other health impairment* means having limited strength, vitality, or alertness, including a heightened alertness to environmental stimuli, that results in limited alertness with respect to the educational environment, that—

> (i) Is due to chronic or acute health problems such as asthma, attention deficit disorder or attention deficit hyperactivity disorder, diabetes, epilepsy, a heart condition, hemophilia, lead poisoning, leukemia, nephritis, rheumatic fever, sickle cell anemia, and Tourette's syndrome; and
>
> (ii) Adversely affects a child's educational performance. (IDEA, 2006, p. 219)

Coding for a Specific Learning Disability—Code #09

Staff and parents may see a disparity between the student's cognitive potential as demonstrated by his verbal or spatial abilities in his area of passion, and his academic weaknesses such as written expression, reading comprehension, and organization. A study by Griswold, Barnhill, Myles, Hagiwara, and Simpson (2002) found that students with AS had lower achievement scores in written expression, listening comprehension, and numerical operations. Although students with AS may respond to some of the instructional interventions used for learning-disabled students, a better understanding of their unique constellation of strengths and needs typically comes from accurate coding under the autism classification. Specific learning disabilities are defined in IDEA as follows:

> *Specific Learning Disability*—(i) *General.* Specific learning disability means a disorder in one or more of the basic psychological processes involved in understanding or in using language, spoken or written, that may manifest itself in the imperfect ability to listen, think, speak, read, write, spell, or to do mathematical calculations, including conditions such as perceptual disabilities, brain injury, minimal brain dysfunction, dyslexia, and developmental aphasia.
>
> (ii) *Disorders not included.* Specific learning disability does not include learning problems that are primarily the result of visual, hearing, or motor disabilities, of mental retarda-

tion, of emotional disturbance, or of environmental, cultural, or economic disadvantage. (IDEA, 2006, p. 219)

Coding as Speech or Language Impaired—Code #04

As discussed earlier in this book, students with AS frequently have difficulties with their pragmatic language, the ability to communicate effectively with others. This language impairment may have a great effect on them in the educational setting. Although most students with AS will need goals and services targeted at improving their communication skills, we believe that it is more appropriate to identify these students as being on the autism spectrum, in order to give staff a complete understanding of their issues. Having said that, there will be times when it is not yet clear that the student should be identified as having AS and qualifying her for services through identification of her speech and language needs may be the best way to initially ensure that she is provided with the services that she needs. Speech and language impairment is defined in IDEA as follows:

> (11) *Speech or language impairment* means a communication disorder, such as stuttering, impaired articulation, a language impairment, or a voice impairment, that adversely affects a child's educational performance. (IDEA, 2006, p. 219)

Practice in inference, abstraction, and pragmatic or functional language are the most common areas of speech/language improvements needed for children with AS.

In summary, students with AS may qualify for special education services through their identification as being labeled with any of a variety of educational disability codes. Although we believe that identifying students with the autism coding is generally the most accurate and helpful identification, regardless of which coding is used the student can qualify for all of the appropriate services that he needs. It is the goals and objectives of the IEP, not the coding, that actually drive the services and placement. The next step toward qualifying for an IEP is to look at whether or not the student's disability impacts his educational progress.

Educational Impact

Once it has been determined that a disability exists, the next step in determining whether or not the student qualifies for an IEP is the consideration of whether or not the student's disability impacts his education. This is often a very difficult decision and can be somewhat contentious. The parents may see the educational impact in the fact that the student is anxious and depressed, is spending long hours outside of school studying in an effort to keep up, and/or that his or her self-esteem is plummeting. School staff may not see the educational impact, as the student may not display his emotional issues during the school day and his grades may be adequate. How to determine educational impact is not defined in the law and is often the source of disagreement at school meetings. Some school officials have described educational impact as including academic impact, as well as other things that may prevent a child from participating in the life of a classroom. This unofficial definition at least opens the door to look beyond grades and test scores to the student's participation in the entire school day. As advocates for students with AS, it is important for parents and teachers to look not only at the data about a student's educational performance, but also to his or her entire experience of the school environment.

As advocates for students with AS, it is important for parents and teachers to look not only at the data about a student's educational performance, but also to his or her entire experience of the school environment.

Determination of FAPE

One of the standards for development of an IEP is that each student's plan be calculated to provide a Free and Appropriate Public Education (FAPE). In the past, FAPE has been described as providing a basic "floor of opportunity," and school systems have often argued that that they are only required by law to provide programs from which the students derive "some educational benefit" (*Board of Education of Hendrick Hudson Central School District, Westchester City v. Rowley*, 1982, p. 200). An important new court decision expands this definition of FAPE to include the requirement that IEPs should be designed to help the student achieve independence and self-sufficiency. Expanding on this concept, a Washington court ruled in 2006 that specific methodologies need to be included in the IEP and that accommodations alone are not sufficient to meet this need (*J. L., M. L. & K. L. v. Mercer Island School District*). Rather than accommodations alone, specially designed instruction for improving the student's skills must be included in each IEP. This court decision is particularly significant for students with AS. The concept that FAPE includes a requirement that IEPs should be aimed at the outcomes of independence and self-sufficiency may open the door to more targeted and comprehensive services for these students. Improved social skills and executive functioning skills certainly are needed by many students with AS, if they are to become independent and self-sufficient.

The IEP

Once the decisions have been made that a student has an educational disability and qualifies for an IEP, goals and objectives are designed to address the student's identified needs. Regardless of the coding, goals and objectives should be designed to address all areas that are in need of improvement. In addition, supplementary aides and services that need to be present in the classroom, as well as accommodations that are needed in test situations, are included in the IEP. When determining appropriate classroom and testing aides and accommodations, it is important to focus on the strengths of the student. For example, a student with strong visual skills could create a web of his ideas, perhaps with the help of computer software, before he begins writing.

Definition of LRE

Finally, a determination is made regarding where the student will receive the services described in his or her IEP. Federal and state laws mandate that each student's needs be met in the Least Restrictive Environment (LRE). However, it is important to remember that what is the Least Restrictive Environment for one student may not meet the needs of another student. On the one hand, the law calls for efforts to be made to educate students with their nondisabled peers. On the other, the law clearly states that if the "nature or severity of the disability is such that education in regular classes with the use of supplementary aids and services cannot be achieved satisfactorily . . ." children with disabilities may be removed from the regular environment (IDEA, 2006, p. 226–227). The law also clearly states that each public agency must ensure that a continuum of alternative placements is available and that these placements include instruction in regular classes with a resource room or itinerant support, special classes, special schools, home instruction, and instruction in hospitals and institutions. Sometimes school officials will argue that to provide the Least Restrictive Environment, a student who is identified as needing special education services must first be served in the regular classroom with supports, and only after this fails can she be considered for a special class or special school placement. We do not believe that this is an accurate interpretation of the law. Instead, we believe that the determination of the LRE is an individual decision regarding what environment is the least restrictive for the student in question for the coming year. This decision, like other IEP decisions, should be reviewed and adjusted on at least a yearly basis, during the mandated annual review. IDEA defines Least Restrictive Environment as follows:

> §300.114 LRE requirements.
>
> (2) Each public agency must ensure that—
>
> > (i) To the maximum extent appropriate, children with disabilities, including children in public or private institutions or other care facilities, are educated with children who are nondisabled; and
> >
> > (ii) Special classes, separate schooling, or other removal of children with disabilities from the regular educational environment occurs only if the nature or severity of the disability is such that education in regular classes with the use of supplementary aids and services cannot be achieved satisfactorily.

> §300.115 Continuum of alternative placements.
>
> > (a) Each public agency must ensure that a continuum of alternative placements is available to meet the needs of children with disabilities for special education and related services.
> >
> > (b) The continuum required in paragraph (a) of this section must—
> >
> > > (1) Include the alternative placements listed in the definition of special education under §300.38 (instruction in regular classes, special classes, spe-

> cial schools, home instruction, and instruction in hospitals and institutions); and
>
> (2) Make provision for supplementary services (such as resource room or itinerant instruction) to be provided in conjunction with regular class placement. (IDEA, 2006, pp. 226–227)

Program Options

As described in the discussion of LRE above, program options for students with AS range from the typical classroom to separate schools, depending on the nature and severity of the student's disability.

Instruction in Regular Classes

Students identified with AS may receive all of their education in the regular classroom. General educators, with consultation from special education teachers and service providers, may provide the needed supplementary aides and accommodations and work on helping students to improve in their areas of weakness. Special educators and service providers may visit the classroom to discretely provide services to the students, without having them miss classroom instruction or be segregated from the life of the classroom.

Instruction in Special Classes

In order to provide special education instruction to the student with AS, it may be beneficial for the special educator or related service provider (speech pathologist, psychologist, counselor, or occupational therapist) to see the student in an individual or small-group session outside of the classroom. This pull-out model allows for specialized instruction to be delivered to the student in an environment where it does not distract others or make the student obviously stand out by having other students observe his special instruction. These special classes are especially important and useful when the instruction that will be provided is different or supplementary to what is being done in the regular class. It also allows for small-group or individual instruction, which may be more beneficial to some students with AS. Many students with AS benefit from receiving the support of a resource room period that serves as a home base where they can receive support with organization, written language, and other academic issues, while also receiving coaching regarding social skills issues.

Special Schools

Some students with AS may not benefit from education in regular classes. For them, the potential harmful effects of removing them from their neighborhood school are outweighed by the benefits of receiving appropriate education throughout the day from a highly trained staff that is knowledgeable about AS and able to provide an environment that incorporates all of the needed interventions, while integrating services throughout the day. Some students are so challenged by mainstream environments that they become easily overwhelmed. These students may require an element of protective emotional safety that may be provided by some separate, special schools. Special schools generally provide a smaller student-to-staff ratio, allowing for greater individualization of specialized instruction.

Alternative School Programs

Some parents may opt to place their children in alternative schools that may or may not be special education schools. These schools may provide an environment for students, with or without disabilities, that is a better match for the strengths and needs of the specific student with AS. Parents are cautioned to make sure that the staff has expertise in working with students with AS and that the methodology that will be employed is truly a good match for their child. These schools differ from the special schools described above in that they are not necessarily state certified in special education.

Homeschooling

Some parents have opted to take their children out of school environments that they perceive as not helpful or possibly harmful and instead provide education for them at home. We believe that this should only be done for students with AS in extreme situations and then, only until a suitable program can be found. One of the primary needs of students with AS is that they work at developing their social skills. Some parents have made the homeschooling environment work for their students by connecting with other homeschoolers to provide regular social activities. There are many homeschooling curricula available for general education, which parents of students with AS can augment by providing opportunities for social interaction and other needed supports in the community. We still feel that it is unusual that parents would have sufficient expertise in the best practices of working with students with AS to be the best educators for their child over the long run.

Home and Hospital Teaching

There may be times in the life of the student with AS when his emotional distress related to his AS becomes so severe that it is in his best interest that he be removed from the school environment. At this time, mental health professionals should work with the student while he is receiving home tutoring or participating in a full or partial day hospitalization to stabilize him, with the goal of returning him to his school placement. There are a small percentage of students with AS who regularly experience a high level of emotional distress for whom home and hospital teaching or hospitalization is periodically required.

Services Available at Different Points Along the "Road"

In conclusion, although we have been focusing on how students with AS may qualify for an IEP and what school services may be provided once they have been identified, it is important to again remember that school services should be provided to a student with AS regardless of whether or not he has been formally identified for a 504 plan or IEP. As parents and teachers move through the process identified on the Road Map (see p. 129), there is an opportunity for the interventions outlined in Chapters 5 and 6 to be employed and adjusted. Beginning with the first parent-teacher conference and continuing on through child-study teams, and potentially beyond into formal plans, interventions should be selected, data should be kept on the effectiveness of the interventions, and meetings should be reconvened to look at whether the interventions need to be continued, modified, or replaced with other, possibly more effective, interventions. Students with AS will be successful in school when parents and school staff work together to select appropriate interventions, continue to dialogue about their effectiveness, and adjust the interventions, service, and school placement accordingly.

chapter 8

Best Practices for Parenting and Raising Kids With AS

AT first, there was denial, then anger, then grief, and finally, gradual acceptance. Even now, years later, some days Kara's parents can accept that their child has Asperger's syndrome and some days they cannot. At first, there was the search for the perfect diagnosis that would explain everything and then provide the magical solution that would cure Kara's problems. Gradually, that was replaced with the understanding that what was important was not so much how her problems or the program where she would go to school were labeled, but whether her education was the right match for her strengths and needs. At first, her parents felt guilt and self-doubt every time there was a new theory regarding a possible cause. Gradually, that was replaced with the acceptance of knowing that there might never be an answer to what was truly the cause of Kara's disorder. At first, there was anger toward the professionals who honestly told them about the challenges that their child faced. Gradually, that was replaced by a desire to make alliances and to work with and trust the professionals who would go above and beyond to see that Kara received appropriate educational services. At first, Kara's parents felt embarrassed that their child was different, less than perfect, and didn't always fit in with others. Gradually, that was replaced with a focus on and celebration of Kara's strengths and a growing desire to challenge others who could only see their little girl's deficits.

One of the biggest problems that you might experience as parents during the early development of children with disabilities, including AS, is confusion over diagnosis. Most parents go to experts for diagnosis and answers about their child. They may obtain the wrong diagnosis or one that is not specific enough. Some experts refuse to use the word *autism* even when it is clear that the criteria apply. Because AS is generally suspected later in a child's developmental stages, it is often confused with many other conditions. And, because the American Psychiatric Association's *DSM-IV* did not feature AS until 1994, the diagnosis was not fully adopted into practice in the professional community until relatively recent times. Still, there is considerable confusion, lack of experience, and lack of standards surrounding AS. You will have difficulty generating accurate expectations when the diagnosis of your child is not clear. In addition, a clear diagnosis allows you to more fully understand the challenges and potential of your child.

As information crystallizes and the diagnostic picture clarifies, there is often a period of bereavement when the child is not what you expected. Often, you must protect yourself to deal with the shock of feeling that your child is "different." This might involve various forms of defensiveness and, frequently, an initial period of denial. There are also problems dealing with public embarrassment when the child is atypical in behavior. There may be the experience of early school rejection, either of being asked to leave a program or not getting admitted to the school you desired for your child.

Problems of speech and language and clumsiness generally are observed first. Before the classification is clear, you might hear a diagnosis of "multisystems disorder," "multihandicapped," "multidisabled," or "developmental delay." Although these general terms are cautious, they often are not made more specific, and these vague labels can last into adolescence without clarity. Psychologists and educators often find themselves reassessing children to clarify the diagnosis along the way.

When facing the stress of dealing with the facts of a child's disability, parents need to be on the same team as one another. You need to discuss your expectations and philosophy of child rearing openly with each other. It is important to try to have complementary or consistent parenting styles. You can't give mixed messages. You need to work in an ongoing fashion in their marital communication and issues. Rearing a child with disabilities can be stressful to any marriage. Very frequently, the couple never seems to have time to take a vacation alone, and many never have a weekend away or even a date for years. Respite through dates and vacations are very important to parents of children with disabilities.

When facing the stress of dealing with the facts of a child's disability, parents need to be on the same team as one another.

Clinical experience and research reflect parents' feelings of guilt when they understandably lose patience with their disabled child (Little, 2002). Protecting yourself against guilt and other forms of parenting stress is part of the adjustment you must experience.

Parents also need to be a team when dealing with the school system. You shouldn't give the school conflicting messages and expectations, argue in front of IEP teams, or create confusion by contacting several different people in the school at once.

Dealing With Your Child's Anxiety

There are several forms of anxiety that parents may observe in their children. One form of anxiety is chronic, which is more hard-wired as a coexisting condition. This is one form of anxiety that may respond best to medication as prescribed by a knowledgeable physician. Social anxiety is part of the fundamental picture of AS, because social coping skills are lacking. Social anxiety responds to a wide range of coordinated treatments, which include direct instruction, or sometimes using such techniques as social stories, scripts, and roleplaying. Anxiety also arises when there is the experience or anticipation of being overwhelmed by too much information, novelty, or complexity. This can happen in the instructional setting in school, the cafeteria, hallways of schools, at the beach, in a mall, or anywhere there is a wide range of intense and unpredictable stimuli. Specific preparation and rehearsal of acquired coping mechanisms may be required.

One of the most challenging forms of anxiety is spiraling anxiety, where the child feels out of control in any of the situations mentioned above. Providing a calming place or activity to help your child gain control of his or her anxiety is a necessity. Some examples of such activities are included in Chapter 6. A simple meditation technique also might be helpful in stabilizing and recentering your child. Many children don't know what it feels like to be calm and at peace. For them, this experience is new and must be learned through a self-modulating experience such as meditation or relaxation therapy.

Dealing With Oppositional Behavior

Rigidity can lead to oppositional resistance under stress as has been described previously. Opposition can be avoided by careful planning, having accurate expectations of how stressors will be addressed, and through planning to ignore the situation when it arises. Rigidity and stubbornness are not necessarily active choices that your child is making. Many children are seen to "lock up" and become oppositional or defiant when faced with stress. Locking up is a way of handling the feeling of being overwhelmed, which stems from the complexity of information or demands for responses your child is experiencing. It is best to provide time for release of the emotion and the frustration that leads to oppositional behavior and the provision of positive consequences for more effective behaviors. Intelligent ignoring, or choosing not to react to negative provocation, and avoiding power struggles always are important and effective tools to use in dealing with opposition. When possible, positive alternative behavior choices should be introduced and reinforced.

Dealing With Tactile Defensiveness

Children with AS are frequently comfortable hugging a parent but few others. This is to be expected. If tactile irritability is present in your child, it is not generally helpful to force physical contact. It is interesting to note that many children with autistic spectrum disorders appear to respond better to deep pressure, such as that used in massage or compression, than they do to more typical, lighter touch.

Handling Social Skills Deficits

Because social skill deficits are at the core of AS, it is understandable that you might experience frustration in helping your child initiate and maintain friendships and avoid peer rejection.

Social clubs and interest groups that match your child's areas of expertise and passion can be helpful. Some afterschool groups are geared to include children with special needs. Children with AS also can act as tutors in the community in areas of their special academic strengths. Social skill therapy groups frequently are geared specifically for children with AS. Much repetition of specific skills may be required. This may involve direct instruction on reading faces and interpreting gestures, and rehearsing and practice of social routines.

Expressing and Reciprocating Affection

Children with AS frequently feel affection but do not know how to appropriately express these feelings. They need to have guidelines as to who is an appropriate recipient of affection and under which conditions. They need to know when someone is a friend or an acquaintance and when intimacy is appropriate.

The first step in reciprocity is simply looking in the direction of the person with whom one is conversing. It is not necessary to look into the other person's eyes in a locked manner at all times. Making eye contact has many cultural variations and implications—although it is expected in many Western societies, in other cultures eye contact has different meanings. For example, in some parts of Asia, the eyes are considered to be the "windows of the soul." There, anger and sexual impulses are believed to be transmitted by staring directly into the eyes. Therefore, direct eye contact, especially between the sexes, is often frowned upon. We suggest that the recipient of eye contact is generally satisfied if the person with whom he or she is conversing looks in the direction of the recipient's face. Many educators and therapist insist on strong eye contact, but this may be culturally insensitive in some cases and very challenging for children with AS. Therefore, we further suggest that the child with AS could be taught to look generally at a point of the "third eye" above and between the eyes in the middle of the forehead. This is a habit with which many persons feel more comfortable. This is a centering and calming experience for both parties, often becoming unconscious with practice. It is important for you to recognize and convey to others that your child's lack of eye contact is not a sign of disrespect and, to some extent, may be difficult to modify.

Teaching Manners

Many children with AS fail to practice good private hygiene behavior. Nose picking, failing to comb hair, and other unhygienic behaviors are not uncommon. Hygiene skills must be directly taught and maintained. Fortunately, these are rule-governed behaviors, which can be memorized.

A Web site called Teacher Planet has a wide range of resources on etiquette for children (visit http://www.teacherplanet.com/resource/manners.php). Some of these resources include visual posters that can be mounted on a wall and used to reinforce good manners. In some areas, consultants are available to teach manners through direct instruction. For example, a class could be taught to model a formal dinner party using proper etiquette, a scenario that would introduce multiple social skills rules to a child with AS without singling him out for his poor manners.

At home, you also can outline and review general rules for good hygiene behavior and manners. You should model to your child what is private hygiene behavior (such as picking one's nose) and what is public hygiene behavior (such as covering one's mouth when coughing). Checklists and rewards and consequences programs also can be implemented to teach these skills.

Dealing With Obsessions

Obsessive interests are a key aspect of AS, and to many, they seem to represent a cognitive strength in children with Asperger's syndrome. Generally, however, obsessive preoccupations interfere with learning other things. Children with AS can be rewarded with time to spend in their area of special interest, as well as materials to use, as a condition of completing assigned, but less desirable, tasks such as homework problems. Their obsessions can be socially embedded or be used in a required social chain of events, such as table games that require taking turns. Vocationally, with some effort, a person with AS can be encouraged to find work that involves her interests in some practical manner.

Children with AS can be rewarded with time to spend in their area of special interest, as well as materials to use, as a condition of completing assigned, but less desirable, tasks such as homework problems.

You should not discount your child's area of interest or obsession, but should monitor and limit the time spent on the interest. Clear rules and boundaries should be described to and enforced to your child as to when she can pursue her obsessions. For example, a parent can set the rule that his child may not work on classifying her latest bug collection specimens during her grandmother's weekly Saturday afternoon visits, but she may be allowed an hour to work independently and without interruption on her interest after Grandma has left, if she displayed proper behavior (also preset by the parent) during the visit. Take caution, however, that children with AS depend on rigidity and scheduled, routine situations, and any planned rules pursuing obsessive interests must be adhered to by the parents. In the above example, if Grandma is sick and cannot visit, the parent should discuss the change in routine with his child and set a new rule (i.e., if the child helps the parent with the household chores during the time that Grandma usually visits, she will still be able to have her quiet time to work on her bug collection).

Managing Attention

Attention problems are among the most common coexisting conditions in AS (there is a minority of cases in which full-blown ADHD is present). Recent studies sponsored by the National Institutes of Mental Health (NIMH) suggest the value of specialized medical consultation in combination with an overall multimodal wraparound plan (Jensen, Hinshaw, & Swanson, 2001).

The key features of ADHD are impulsivity, motor restlessness, and inattention. Generally, ADHD is a problem of restraint, inhibition, and self-modulation. It is about the sustenance of effort and motivation as much as it is about attention problems. We direct readers to the work of Drs. Russell Barkley, Keith Conners, Sam Goldstein, and Mel Levine for good explanations of the diagnosis, treatment, behavior management, and education of students with ADHD. At this point, the research on the topic is voluminous. ADHD was the last "big thing" prior to AS. What is clear from research, especially from the massive, groundbreaking NIMH study (Jensen et al., 2001), is that ADHD should be treated with multiple approaches or a multimodal approach.

The following are elements of such a plan for the child with attention deficits with or without hyperactivity.

1. Accurate assessment is utilized, including medical, neurological, psychiatric, psychological, neuropsychological, social, family systems, educational, and other assessments as needed. Medical conditions such as thyroid dysfunction and allergies should be ruled out.

2. The child's strengths should be identified. It is very important to approach ADHD with a strengths model, because 50–70% of children with ADHD display negative behaviors that can be irritating to parents and teachers. The child with ADHD needs to be "framed" and "reframed" conceptually in a positive manner. This strengths model is effective, because it is the child's strengths that eventually carry his self-esteem and self-concept forward.
3. Parent education is provided, including books, films, lecture series, seminars, parent training programs, and association membership. For example, a wide variety of materials, activities, and other supports may be found by consulting the organization called Children and Adults with Attention Deficit Disorders (CHADD).
4. Parent counseling regarding child management may be required with checkups as needed. An attempt is made to maximize consistency between significant adults in the child's life in philosophy and techniques of child rearing. Parenting stress is evaluated.
5. Medical monitoring of the kind and level of prescription medication (if prescribed) is provided by qualified medical personnel.
6. Case management is assigned to someone (e.g., therapist, school counselor, special educator, school nurse), who communicates with all relevant parties regarding medications and preplanned intervention strategies. Parents frequently contact several school officials at once. It is more effective for all involved to have one pivotal person in the school to maintain ongoing contact.
7. A 504 school plan may be developed with accommodations. Special education coding as other health impaired may be established through special education eligibility meetings under federal law (see the discussion of coding, IEPs, and 504

plans in Chapter 7). If possible, the child should be coached to attend these meetings and to take ownership of the main objectives. Keep the number of objectives prioritized, few, and simple.

8. A school/home contract is used to monitor schoolwork and homework. A school class-by-class monitoring sheet may be necessary with home consequences for compliance. Classwork, homework, and organizational skill objectives may be identified as requirements for each subject. Monitor effectiveness of strategies through periodic teacher and parent ratings of attention, activity level, and related personality/behavior variables. Children may be rewarded at home for positive school ratings. Again, keep the number of objectives down, from three to five at a time.
9. Environmental stress factors are assessed. Stressors at school and home should be identified. Family stress reduction activities are selected and employed by parents, including respite opportunities and vacations.
10. Individual and/or group counseling for the child focuses on self-evaluation, self-monitoring, and educational self-advocacy. Peer relations and self-esteem issues are addressed. This is important because of the high rates of peer rejection experienced by children with ADHD.
11. The child's diet is reviewed for basic good nutrition.
12. Calming and relaxation techniques are explored. These practices include yoga, meditation, and relaxation therapies. While they may not be curative in themselves, they can be helpful to an overall treatment plan. The child needs to learn what being calm feels like as a base experience.
13. Teacher support is provided regarding management, class environment factors, accommodations, and teaching techniques appropriate for the child. The child needs and will

respond to some of the techniques successfully used with children with attention deficits.

Counseling and Psychotherapy

AS is a disability that responds to a multimodal treatment system employing integrated treatments and stakeholders in wraparound systems. In such systems, most aspects of the child's life are addressed with the same general focus on targeted developmental or behavioral objectives. Although each person with AS does not require a wraparound intervention system, multiple treatments often work in combination to make a difference. Sofronoff, Leslie, and Brown (2004) found that combined Cognitive-Behavioral Therapy (CBT) and increased parent involvement helped to reduce anxiety in children with Asperger's. CBT is a very popular form of treatment that involves strengthening conscious verbal control over behavior through review, planning, and rehearsal of specific skills. Klin and colleagues (2000) recommend that AS be treated using an experienced multidisciplinary team. The following components are recommended: (a) a thorough developmental and health history, (b) psychological and communication assessments, and (c) a diagnostic examination including differential diagnosis. Further consultation regarding behavioral management, motor disabilities, possible neurological concerns, psychopharmacology, and assessments related to advanced studies or vocational training are necessary. Wymbs et al. (2005) reported the potential efficacy of long-term, intensive, multimodal treatment using a behavioral summer treatment program, parent and teacher training, and medication.

Talk therapies, especially coaching, parent support, and, in some cases, medications, work together with school and community supports to ensure a safer, healthier, and happier path for the child with AS. Tony Attwood (2004) has developed a modified CBT, called the Emotional Toolbox, to be used in cognitive restructuring, a way of reframing assumptions and interpretations that lead to mood disorders.

Ideally, individual counseling should consist of attempts to use available self-introspective resources, making talking to one's self accurately reflective. This involves learning one's strengths and weaknesses. The goal is to be able to advocate effectively for one's self in a variety of environments. For younger children, self-advocacy also involves methods for dealing with teasing and bullying. Another purpose of self-reflection is learning to be accurate about how to interpret and react to actual problem solving in real-world situations.

In order to know one's self, one needs to know the language of emotions. This includes being able to use labels for feelings. Many people with AS do not distinguish their feelings well and do not have these labels. Feeling words may need to be taught directly. We have found that counseling groups have had some effect when a mental health professional and speech/language therapist work together in a group therapy setting, because social communication is a total package of skills involving both disciplines. It is important to note that talk therapies may not be effective alone or at all when the language and emotional systems are lacking. Generally, a coaching technique such as the one described below is more effective.

Counseling may consist of direct instruction of rules and scripts for interfacing with daily situations. This approach has been referred to as *coaching*. It has been used most recently in working with persons with executive functioning problems. For children with AS, it cannot be assumed that solutions to daily life situations can be generalized. Therefore, it is better to be safe by rehearsing anticipated daily glitches. Other potentially difficult situations, such as planning for local travel, should be rehearsed. Coaching is most valuable in preparation for social interactions.

Vocational exploration, training, and monitoring of employment are also important roles in coaching.

Encouraging Achievement

Often, students' poor school performance may not be related to their disability alone—they also may be displaying underachievement. Frequently, we may be so careful to ensure protections for children with disabilities that we fail to set high standards for them. We should look at the great achievements made by persons like Helen Keller who have displayed high achievement against great odds. We are not suggesting that children should be pushed beyond their limits. Many persons unfamiliar with the complexities of special education issues may oversimplify problems with achievement by suggesting that "if she worked harder, she would be fine." Underachievement can be a problem at all ability levels, whether students are disabled or not. It is important to remember that adults are responsible to some extent for their own happiness, but children require emotional protection and have a right to experience happiness. They also require moral, character, and spiritual guidance to make positive life choices. Commonly assumed markers of achievement should not violate their rights for emotional protection, the experience of happiness, or the ability to think for themselves about their life purposes.

You can encourage your child's achievement in a variety of ways, described in the next few sections.

Home-Related Achievement Issues

Parental attitude in the home is key to encouraging school achievement. We hope we love our children unconditionally, but every child can be frustrating at times. For that reason, parents need to continually evaluate their feelings toward their child.

At times, you may harbor feelings of rejection toward your child, which in turn are responsible for guilty feelings and irrational responses to the guilt. Are there barriers to maintaining and demonstrating unconditional love? Aim at conveying unconditional love to your child as much as possible, even when you are arguing, correcting behavior, or praising them. You should remember that your child's behavior might be bad, but the child isn't. For too many children, shame results from feeling as though they are fundamentally bad. Shame, even for short periods, is one of the most destructive emotions a child can feel. Making a child with disabilities feel shame for something out of his control is abusive. There are parents whose ability to love their child is temporarily blocked due to their own concerns, anxieties, and frustrations. This is, in some way, to be expected when one is rearing a child with AS. Honesty with one's self is very important. There is no perfect way to feel about the situation. Just remember that love emerges when the truth is confronted honestly.

Aim at conveying unconditional love to your child as much as possible, even when you are arguing, correcting behavior, or praising them.

Every child can be seen as a unique gift with unique potential. Avoid comparing your child to other children. Let your child know that you see him as having a duty to know his own strengths and make his best efforts in and out of the classroom. Not every child can be the best at everything, but he can be his best at something. Many very competent children have low expectations for themselves because the bar has been set too low. This is especially the case in children with disabilities—too many parents are happy to see their children just getting by. If your child is currently an underachiever, convey your firm belief and expectation that she can learn and excel. By being a reasonable advocate, be sure that accommodations, supports, and special instructional strategies are in place to make learning easier, but do not relieve your child from her responsibility to make reasonable

Eventually, a child's strengths will emerge, coalesce, and integrate into a unique mix that many parents find they enjoy and treasure.

efforts. Know your child's strengths and weaknesses accurately as they emerge. Eventually, a child's strengths will emerge, coalesce, and integrate into a unique mix that many parents find they enjoy and treasure.

Decrease marital and family conflict that can cause roadblocks and resistance to emotional growth and motivation to learn. Talk with your adult partner about your views and expectations of your child and your family priorities. Never argue about your child in front of your child. Seek to maximize points of agreement and learn to agree where you disagree. Put the "small stuff" aside. Make your discussions a safe place to forge a shared philosophy about child rearing. Try to be on the same page as much as possible about child rearing practices, rules, and consequences. When there are great disparities between parental expectations, children lock up or learn to fail as a way to passively punish parents for not communicating effectively.

Other home-related ideas for encouraging achievement include:

- Provide a sense of harmony in the home that fosters a desire to be there. Try to eat one meal together daily as a family and plan at-home family events such as regular game or movie nights.
- Success feels good. Children are born loving to learn and master challenges. Reward your child's successes with praise in a meaningful and genuine way so that children learn to know the feeling derived from mastering their challenges. Intrinsic incentives often are higher and more enduring rewards than prizes.
- Be patient with your child. A positive self-concept as a learner takes time for a child who has been experiencing little suc-

cess. It may take a while before the positive experience of academic success takes hold.

- Limit television and video game time to one hour per weekday and 1½ hours per weekend day. You should also limit telephone, instant messaging, and computer time.
- Make sure your child gets adequate sleep by turning in nightly at a reasonable hour. Try not to break this rule on the weekends.
- Be open to mental health consultation for significant problems and to receiving parenting counseling. Attend support groups where available or help create one in your area.
- Make sure your child knows the rules for home behavior and responsibilities. Have them written out and posted in the child's room until she has mastered them.
- Develop a "To Do" list to post inside your child's bedroom door with a check-off system. You may want to update this weekly as your child receives assignments from school, or even daily.
- Remember that children see structure and limits as part of being loved. They are uncomfortable, confused, and even frightened without clear limits and expectations.
- Be a benevolent dictator first, and a friend later, when rules are established. Freedom should be earned through demonstrated responsibility.
- Model the behavior and values you expect from your child in your own day-to-day activities, behavior, and conversation.
- Regularly demonstrate affection, especially with teenagers. Tell your child you love him regularly.
- Evaluate the openness of your communication with your child through regular conversations. Children need to feel your benign presence and acceptance through regular communication.

School-Related Achievement Issues

As a parent of a child with a disability, you should be in regular contact with your child's school. Try to keep one teacher, special educator, administrator, or counselor as a pivotal information conduit. Use voicemail, e-mail, or any form of communication that is convenient for the school representative, and always communicate on an agreed-upon schedule for setting up meetings about your child. Establish good communication boundaries with your school representative and stick to them.

Parents should also set up homework rules and guidelines. Agree with your child on regular study times every day for homework. Break up homework periods with dinner, snack, or exercise breaks. Also be sure to encourage your child to communicate about homework problems or questions with friends through telephone, instant messaging, or study groups.

A parent's attitude toward school can make all the difference in a child's achievement. Convey to your child that school is an honorable place, that teachers are worthy of respect, and that school achievement is their major job, second only to being a good human being. Volunteer to help out at school at least once a month, even with (or especially with) menial tasks. Let the school teacher or staff members provide you with the work they need done. Volunteering should be controlled by the school and not by the parents' ideas of what the school needs. Volunteering at your child's school will show her that you value school as a part of your community.

Convey to your child that school is an honorable place, that teachers are worthy of respect, and that school achievement is their major job, second only to being a good human being.

Other ideas for improving school achievement at home include:

- Attend at least one PTA or school function quarterly.
- Never miss a Back to School Night or teacher/parent conference.
- Find validity about your child's needs by obtaining solid data. This might be supplied by regular school testing or individualized psychological and/or educational assessments.
- Home responsibilities and chores are important, but should take second place to homework.
- At night place everything needed for the next day's schoolwork next to the front door (or back) in your child's backpack, so it can't be forgotten the next morning.
- Check that your child has homework. If your child is lying about homework, that is still a lie and a serious problem, even if it is a little lie.
- Read to or with your young child every night. And, let your child see you reading at home.
- Develop a timetable for improved grades.
- Directly explain the importance of good grades as a pathway to achievement in obtaining life's long-term rewards.
- Encourage your child to be unafraid to associate with and play with high-achieving children. You have a right to express your approval or concern about your child's friends.
- Encourage your child to have extracurricular activities at school. Concentrate on activities that your child actually enjoys to make school a desirable place to be.

Overall, remember that parents are their child's first and most important teachers. Parenting is a great art, as well as responsibility. Parents do play a key role in helping children adjust and master their worlds. This can be particularly challenging when the symptoms of AS inhibit practical, functional daily adjustment. Parents are to be commended for their efforts, flexibility, perseverance, and creativity in child rearing with kids who present challenges. They need to also realize that they cannot do it all alone and need to network, utilize, and create community supports for their children.

chapter 9

Other Experiences: College, Work, and Independent Living

WHAT a relief and a joy it was to see Ben's acceptance into the University of Miami as a transfer student for his junior year of college. He would be majoring in engineering, his area of interest, passion, and talent. His 2 years at Brevard Community College in Florida had been extremely successful. Working closely with the school's disabilities coordinator, Ben had drafted a letter to each of his professors at the beginning of each semester telling them that he had AS and describing his unique strengths and needs. These teachers, who had been handpicked by the disabilities coordinator, were very receptive to allowing any and all of the accommodations that Ben might need, such as always giving instruction, directions, and assignments visually. Just knowing that he could stop in and see the disabilities coordinator for support had been a great relief to Ben, as well. Despite all of Ben's success, his future still remained somewhat uncertain. He clearly still needed support with social skills and, although he had learned to take care of himself, he still preferred to live at home. He would continue to face great challenges as he went forward into his years at the University of Miami and beyond into his career and independent adult life.

AS is a lifelong condition; it does not end when formal schooling is completed. We have stated earlier the dangers of failing to diagnose AS early and accurately and many of the negative experiences suffered by adults whose needs have never been adequately addressed. With appropriate intervention and planning, individuals with AS can go on to be successful in post-secondary education and satisfying careers.

College Planning

College administrators have begun to hold regional and national conferences about accommodating for the increase of students with AS and high-functioning autism. Best practices are just being developed. Soon, increasing successes will be seen through graduation and other outcome measures that will demonstrate if new college programs and accommodations are working.

Having IEPs and 504 plans and being prepared to advocate for themselves, many students with AS are now are taking on the challenge of higher education.

Community colleges are particularly affected by an influx of students with AS. Many students are hesitant about their ability to handle 4 years of college. However, many AS students would have been fearful of attending any college in the past. Having IEPs and 504 plans and being prepared to advocate for themselves, many students with AS are now are taking on the challenge of higher education. Students with AS need different supports than have been available to students with learning disabilities in the past. Just as in any previous part of the learning process, highly individualized programs and supports are required for each student.

The TEACCH centers of North Carolina are long-standing multiservice centers for persons with autism. A program of support developed by Ann Palmer and Gladys Williams of the Chapel Hill TEACCH Center works with students with high-functioning autism or AS considering or attending college. Their work provides detailed information on selecting a college, precollege planning, academic support and accommodations, organization, selecting courses, social life, living in the dorms, and daily living. One promising resource for students with AS planning to attend college is a book called *Realizing the College Dream With Autism or Asperger Syndrome* (Palmer, 2005), which provides advice on how to get into college and how to adjust to the college lifestyle and educational demands.

Another promising program for college students with AS is the College Internship Program (M. McManmon, personal communication, December 2006). Located near several college campuses, this program provides all of the auxiliary services that help students to negotiate college life. Students are supported with all phases of college and independent living, including interviewing for college admission and jobs, finding jobs and internships, locating their classes on campus, developing budgeting and banking skills, learning problem-solving skills, maintaining an apartment and car, maintaining physical fitness and heath, navigating dating and social relationships, planning for travel and other transportation, and seeking out counseling and group therapy as needed.

Independent Living

Life for adults with AS without early diagnosis and preparation can be a struggle. Engström, Ekström, and Emilsson (2003), in a Swedish study of adult adjustment, reported that the majority of their subjects were living independently, and all but one was unemployed. None were married and none had children. Only a few had a partner. Most persons needed a high level of public and/or private support. The overall adjustment was rated good in 12%, fair in 75%, and poor in 12% of the population studied. The authors concluded that persons with AS and HFA have extensive need for support from their families and society. We have mentioned earlier that there are legal and psychiatric risks for adults who have not had proper diagnosis and supports throughout their lives. Because AS is only recently being recognized and standardized as a diagnostic category, there are many adults in their 40s and older who have not benefited from the recent explosion of interest and knowledge in this area.

Employment and Work Opportunities

Many of the manifestations found in the diagnostic classification of AS can be translated into work behaviors or preferences. Table 1 provides a list of these behaviors.

There have been very few studies on supported employment for adults, although it is clear that these supports are beneficial, and, in many cases, necessary. Howlin, Alcock, and Burkin (2005) conducted an 8-year follow-up of a specialist supported employment service for high-ability adults with autism or AS. Of the 192 jobs available, approximately 68% of the clients found employment. The majority was hired on permanent contracts and most involved administrative, technical, or computing

Table 1

Here are some work-related problems taken from the social characteristics list by Roger Meyer and Tony Attwood (2001) often faced by persons with AS:

- Difficulty with teamwork.
- Deliberate withholding of peak performance due to belief that one's best efforts may remain unrecognized, unrewarded, or appropriated by others.
- Intense pride in expertise or performance, often perceived by others as "flouting behavior."
- Sarcasm, negativism, criticism.
- Difficulty in accepting compliments, often responding with quizzical or self-deprecatory language.
- Tendency to lose it during sensory overload, multitask demands, or when contradictory and confusing priorities have been set.
- Difficulty in starting projects.
- Discomfort with competition, out of scale reactions to losing.
- Low motivation to perform tasks of no immediate personal interest.
- Oversight or forgetting of tasks without formal reminders such as lists or schedules.
- Great concern about order and appearance of personal work area.
- Slow performance.
- Perfectionism.
- Difficulty with unstructured time.
- Reluctance to ask for help or seek comfort.

- Excessive questions.
- Low sensitivity to risks in the environment to self and/or others.
- Difficulty with writing and reports.
- Reliance on internal speech process to talk oneself through a task or procedure.
- Stress, frustration, and angry reaction to interruptions.
- Difficulty in negotiating, either in conflict situations or as a self-advocate.
- Very low level of assertiveness.
- Reluctance to accept positions of authority or supervision.
- Strong desire to coach or mentor newcomers.
- Difficulty in handling relationships with authority figures.
- Often viewed as vulnerable or less able to resist harassment and badgering by others.
- Punctual and conscientious.
- Avoids socializing, "hanging out," or small talk on and off the job. (Meyer & Attwood, 2001, p. 306)

work. This program was for clients with IQs of 60 and above. Work was also found for lower functioning persons. Individuals supported by the program showed a rise in salaries, contributed more taxes, and claimed fewer benefits. Satisfaction with the scheme was rated highly among clients, employers, and support workers. Moreover, there were many nonfinancial benefits.

Without supervision in vocational planning and on-the-job training and coaching, the outcomes may not be as promising. For example, Hurlbutt and Chalmers (2004) followed six adults, all of whom had difficulty finding work that was commensurate with their ability levels and had difficulty maintaining jobs. Nesbitt (2000) found in a study of 29 organizations employing adults with AS and 40 organizations not employing adults with AS that organizations that did not employ these adults focused on competency expectations, while employers who did hire adults with AS utilized information about the disorder and support from professionals. It is clear that an educated and supported employer is very helpful, if not absolutely necessary, for many adults with AS.

Assessment of Adults

Currently, tests for adults are being developed or refined partially because so many persons with AS aren't being identified until adulthood. These instruments include such measures as the Empathy Quotient (Baron-Cohen & Wheelwright, 2004), the Friendship Questionnaire (Baron-Cohen & Wheelwright, 2003), and others such as the Adult Asperger Syndrome Scale (AASS; Foster, 2003) and the Autism-Spectrum Quotient (AQ) by Woodbury-Smith, Robinson, Wheelwright, and Baron-Cohen (2005). Depending on the individual, a comprehensive assessment battery may be required. In addition to a comprehensive history, interviews, and AS rating scales, assessment may include IQ, personality, projective, achievement, perceptual, motor, attention, neuropsychological, adaptive, and career interest testing. Frequently, young adult college students with AS are asked for permission to obtain interviews and ratings from their parents.

We have referred to mental health concerns in undiagnosed adults. Raja and Azzoni (2001) found 1 in 500 persons who were admitted to a psychiatric hospital in Rome met the diagnostic criteria for AS. It was not unusual for schizophrenia to be expected in these diagnoses. Tantam (2000) described secondary reactions to the stress of coping with the disability socially, which included affective disorders, anxiety-related disorders, and conduct disorders. Marston and Clarke (1999) have addressed the problems of grief and bereavement experienced when a person with AS is faced with the loss of a loved one. Death is part of life as is mourning. When individuals struggle with identifying and expressing emotions, the bereavement process can be difficult.

Parents of children with AS must use a great deal of foresight and planning to prepare and protect their children for the challenges of adulthood.

Parents of children with AS must use a great deal of foresight and planning to prepare and protect their children for the challenges of adulthood. This includes planning for financial and related arrangements. Increasingly, you can find attorneys specializing in establishing trust funds and other unique legal and financial arrangements to protect children with AS as their parents age.

The transition planning process in the U.S. should start by age 14, when transition planning begins in the public schools for those students who qualify with a disability under special education law. Many programs with high school curricula are only beginning to build robust and aggressive programs of post-secondary adult integration into society for the world of work and independent living. State agencies, which have had greater familiarity with low-functioning children with developmental disabilities, have begun to adjust to the increases in the number of persons diagnosed with AS.

Increasingly, adults with AS are forming their own coalitions and other groups to support themselves and develop their own sense of community. This includes the establishment of members-only Web sites, chat rooms, and clubs, and even living arrangements.

It is hoped that the future holds greater openness to the inclusion of persons with AS in the workplace, and that persons with AS will feel increasingly comfortable and effective in society as a whole.

chapter 10

School Success for Kids With AS

SUE Klingshirn, autism consultant for the Medina City School District in Ohio, first met Ethan when he was in fourth grade. His classroom teachers were reporting his inability to begin work and stay on task, his lack of organization, and his problems with social skills. After Ethan was identified as needing an IEP in another school district, Ethan and his family relocated to the Medina City School District, where his parents believed he would receive the educational support he needed. Sue included Ethan in a social skills group with other students at the elementary school. Ethan had a focused interest (some would call it an obsession) with cleaning. An individual contract was set up with Ethan where he could earn the "privilege" of cleaning Sue's room at the end of the day if he completed his class work with a certain number of prompts. Needless to say, Sue was very happy when Ethan met his goal!

Throughout middle school, Ethan progressed with the guidance and support of several wonderful special education teachers who received extra training and consultation from Sue and others on working with students who have AS. During this critical period of social development, Sue worked on social skills with Ethan three times a week. He was included in a group with two other students with AS. Neurotypical peers were brought in on a regular basis to help the students with AS with specific middle school social issues. For example, when a school dance was approaching, three girls worked with Ethan and his peer group on where to go, what to do, what to wear, and all the other "rules" of this social event. They even brought in examples of the music that would be played so that Ethan and the others would have a chance to get used to it. At other times during the year, the group practiced making phone calls to peers and talking to others about school and homework. Ethan learned the rules of meeting new people and entering into existing conversations. Beginning in eighth grade, Ethan began visiting the high school once a month to prepare for that huge transition.

Now in ninth grade, Ethan has done very well in his new school. He uses a laptop computer for his class work and is now able to take his own notes. The older he gets, the fewer modifications he needs and receives. He is able to finish tests now with one extra class period. (In middle school, he once took 3 days to complete a test!) Ethan's teachers are trained in working with students with AS and receive support from Sue and other special educators in the school. Ethan responds very well to the wait time, visual accommodations, and organization structures that teachers use throughout his day. Ethan has clearly benefited from his daily social skills class where he's learning the skills of how to work cooperatively in a team or group situation, how to deal with bullying, and how to navigate the world of dating. Ethan continues to work on improving his self-advocacy skills. One successful strategy has been for him to mark an "H" on any paper with which he is having difficulty, so that he can remember to ask for help later in the day, from one of his special educators. Ethan also reports that he has had a hard time making friends. He says that in the past he may have talked too much or not asked the other person enough questions. Although he is happy to have one trusted friend, he says it's difficult to make others because they may not be interested in his interests, which include cleaning and yard work and tractors and trucks.

However, Ethan has come a long way since Sue met him in fourth grade. She feels that this has been a result of teamwork between his home and school environments. Sue talks about the fact that Ethan's parents have high expectations for him and advocate for what he needs, while always keeping in mind the big picture of moving him from dependence to independence over time (S. Klingshirn, personal communication, February 2007).

It's easy to imagine, from Ethan's example, that Sue Klingshirn works tirelessly to make sure that all students with AS can successfully participate in their neighborhood high school, a high school that serves 2,400 students. Sue has put a system in place that educates and supports staff so that students with AS can have their needs met in their classrooms throughout the day. She identifies general education staff members at each grade level who take the lead in providing appropriate education for these students. These designated teachers participate in training in order to learn about students with AS. Sue meets formally with all of these teachers every 2 weeks and is available for quick consultations on a daily basis. Dealing with sensory issues, as well as behavioral issues, are frequent topics of discussion in these meetings. In addition to Sue, an occupational therapist and a school psychologist typically attend these meetings and help solve problems and provide training. In addition to providing training to classroom teachers, all school staff in Medina City, including secretaries and bus drivers, also receive periodic training on the characteristics of students with

AS, as well as the best practices for working with this special group of kids.

Classroom teachers learn that it is crucial to use visual supports for these students. They provide visual supports in their classes by always being sure to post the agenda for the day on the board, providing clear written instructions and directions, using colors to differentiate and designate important materials and concepts, and incorporating routines as simple as holding up the book or material to which they are orally referring. Sue says that if you ask the teachers about the most important accommodation that they use, most will speak about "wait time," or allowing each student time to process the question and information before responding. Interestingly, teachers report that the accommodations that are good for kids with AS also help many of the other kids, as well.

Students with AS in the Medina City program follow a typical schedule for a majority of their day. When needed, special education teachers may be in the general education classroom to coteach or to be available to support the students with AS. One important addition to the students' schedule is a special health class taught by an exceptional physical education teacher. In a small classroom environment, students work on social skills and school survival skills, as well as participate in adapted physical education activities with a limited number of neurotypical peers.

The success of Sue's program is not only due to the supports that students with AS receive once they enter high school, it is a culmination of work that has been done with the students since they were in elementary school. There is a careful transition put into place to prepare students to move from elementary to middle school and then from middle school to high school. After participating in prep time in their middle school, eighth-grade students with AS come to the high school once a month. They learn to navigate the halls, eat lunch in the crowded and noisy cafeteria, learn the locations of the classes that they will take upon arriving in high school, and even gain experience with these classes by sitting in on them.

The Medina City Asperger's program is one outstanding example of a school program that supports students with AS. Whether students are supported in the general education program, as described in the example of the Medina City program; whether they are attending special classes within a general education school, as described in the example of the Montgomery County program in Chapter 6; or whether they are attending special schools, as described in the example of the Ivymount School in Chapter 7, it is crucial that school staff members are trained in the best practices for educating this population.

When educators and parents work as a team, employing the best practices described in this book in the best interests of students with AS, it is clear that these students can and will experience school success. Asperger's syndrome has no cure, but with the use of proper supports and strategies in the home and school environment to help them overcome their weaknesses and build their confidence as successful students, individuals with AS can live happy, successful lives. The intensity of supports afforded each individual will vary. Although students with AS face significant challenges, with early and effective intervention, they can be expected to live lives that are personally satisfying and that make contributions to our society as a whole.

Asperger's syndrome has no cure, but with the use of proper supports and strategies in the home and school environment to help them overcome their weaknesses and build their confidence as successful students, individuals with AS can live happy, successful lives.

References

American Psychiatric Association. (1994). *Diagnostic and statistical manual of mental disorders–IV*. Washington, DC: Author.

Asperger, H. (1944). Die 'autistischen psychopathen' im kindesalter. *Archiv für Psychiatrie und Nervenkrankheiten, 117*, 76–136.

Attwood, T. (1996). *Asperger's syndrome: A guide for parents and professionals*. Philadelphia: Jessica Kingsley.

Attwood, T. (2004). Cognitive behaviour therapy for children and adults with Asperger syndrome. *Behaviour Change, 21*, 147–161.

Baron-Cohen S., Baldwin, D. A., & Crowson M. (1997, February). Do children with autism use the speaker's direction of gaze strategy to crack the code of language? *Child Development, 68*, 48–57.

Baron-Cohen, S., O'Riordan, M., Stone, V., Jones, R., & Plaisted, K. (1999). Recognition of faux pas by normally developing children and children with Asperger syndrome or high-functioning autism. *Journal of Autism and Developmental Disorders, 29*, 407–418.

Baron-Cohen, S., & Wheelwright, S. (2003). The friendship questionnaire: An investigation of adults with Asperger syndrome or high-functioning autism, and normal sex differences. *Journal of Autism and Developmental Disorders, 33*, 509–517.

Baron-Cohen, S., & Wheelwright, S. (2004). The empathy quotient (EQ): An investigation of adults with Asperger syndrome or high functioning autism, and normal sex differences. *Journal of Autism and Developmental Disorders, 34*, 163–175.

Barton, J. J. S., Cherkasova, M. V., Hefter, R., Cox, T. A., O'Connor, M., & Manoach, D. S. (2004). Are patients with social developmental disorders prosopagnosic? Perceptual heterogeneity in the Asperger and socio-emotional processing disorders. *Brain, 127*, 1706–1716.

Behar, D. (1998). Bipolar overdiagnosis [Letter to the editor]. *Clinical Psychiatry News, 26*(11), 20.

Blackshaw, A. J., Kinderman, P., Hare, D. J., & Hatton, C . (2001). Theory of mind, causal attribution and paranoia in Asperger syndrome. *Autism, 5*, 147–163.

Board of Education of Hendrick Hudson Central School District, Westchester City v. Rowley, 458 U.S. 176 (1982).

Bock, M. A. (2001). SODA strategy: Enhancing the social interaction skills of youngsters. *Intervention in School and Clinic, 36*, 272–278.

Campbell, J. M. (2005). Diagnostic assessment of children with Asperger's disorder: A review of five third-party rating scales. *Journal of Autism and Developmental Disorders, 35*, 25–35.

Castelli, F., Frith, C., Happé, F., & Frith, U. (2002). Autism, Asperger syndrome and brain mechanisms for the attribution of mental states to animated shapes. *Brain, 125*, 1839–1849.

Carrington, S., Templeton, E., & Papinczak, T. (2003). Adolescents with Asperger syndrome and perceptions of friendship. *Focus on Autism and Other Developmental Disabilities, 18*, 211–218.

Centers for Disease Control and Prevention. (n.d.). *Prevalence of the autism spectrum disorders in multiple areas of the United States, surveillance years 2000 and 2002: A report from the autism and developmental disabilities monitoring (ADDM) network*. Retrieved February 19, 2007, from http://www.cdc.gov/ncbddd/dd/addmprevalence.htm

Charman, T., Howlin, P., Berry, B., & Prince, E. (2004). Measuring developmental progress of children with autistic spectrum disorder on school entry using parental report. *Autism, 8*, 89–100.

Coucouvanis, J. (2005). *Super skills: A social skills program for students with Asperger syndrome, high functioning autism and related challenges*. Shawnee Mission, KS: Autism Asperger Publishing.

Craig, J. S., Hatton, C., Craig, F. B., & Bentall, R. P. (2004). Persecutory beliefs, attributions and theory of mind: Comparison of patients with paranoid delusions, Asperger's syndrome and healthy controls. *Schizophrenia Research, 69*, 29–33.

Critchley, H. D., Daly, E. M., Bullmore, E. T., Williams, S., Van Amelsvoort, T., Robertson, D. M., et al. (2000). The functional neuroanatomy of social behaviour: Changes in cerebral blood flow when people with autistic disorder process facial expressions. *Brain, 123*, 2203–2212.

Denckla, M. (1994). Measurement of executive function. In G. R. Lyon (Ed.), *Frames of reference for the assessment of learning disabilities: New views on measurement issues* (pp. 117–142). Baltimore: Paul H. Brookes.

Deruelle, C., Rondan, C., Gepner, B., & Tardif, C. (2004). Spatial frequency and face processing in children with autism and Asperger syndrome. *Journal of Autism and Developmental Disorders, 34*, 199–210.

Dunn, W., Myles B. S., & Orr, S. (2002). Sensory processing issues associated with Asperger syndrome: A preliminary investigation. *American Journal of Occupational Therapy, 56*, 97–102.

Durand, C. M., Betancur, C., Boeckers, T. M., Bockmann, J., Chaste, P., & Fauchereau, F. (2006). Mutations in the gene encoding the synaptic scaffolding protein SHANK3 are associated with autism spectrum disorders. *Nature Genetics, 39*, 25–27.

Eagle, R. S. (2004). Further commentary on the debate regarding increase in autism in California. *Journal of Autism and Developmental Disorders, 34*, 87–88.

Engström, I., Ekström, L., & Emilsson, B. (2003). Psychosocial functioning in a group of Swedish adults with Asperger syndrome or high-functioning autism. *Autism, 7*, 99–110.

Ferguson, H., Myles, B. S., & Hagiwara, T. (2005). Using a personal digital assistant to enhance the independence of an adolescent with Asperger syndrome. *Education and Training in Developmental Disabilities, 40*, 60–67.

Fitzgerald, M., & Bellgrove, M. (2006). The overlap between alexithymia and Asperger's syndrome. *Journal of Autism and Developmental Disorders, 36*, 573–576.

Fombonne, E. (2003). Epidemiological surveys of autism and other pervasive developmental disorders: An update. *Journal of Autism and Developmental Disorders, 33*, 365–382.

Fombonne, E., & Tidmarsh, L. (2003). Epidemiologic data on Asperger disorder. *Child and Adolescent Psychiatric Clinics of North America, 12*, 15–21.

Foster, M. A. (2003). The development of the Adult Asperger Syndrome Scale. *Dissertation Abstracts International, 64*(6-B), 2915.

Frith, U. (1991). Asperger and his syndrome. In U. Frith (Ed.), *Autism and Asperger syndrome* (pp. 1–36). Cambridge, UK: Cambridge University Press.

Ghaziuddin, M., & Gerstein, L. (1996). Pedantic speaking style differentiates Asperger syndrome from high-functioning autism. *Journal of Autism and Developmental Disorders, 26*, 585–595.

Ghaziuddin, M., & Mountain-Kimchi, K. (2004). Defining the intellectual profile of Asperger syndrome: Comparison with high-functioning autism. *Journal of Autism and Developmental Disorders, 34*, 279–284.

Ghaziuddin, M. G., Tsai, L. T., & Ghaziuddin, N. (1992). A reappraisal of clumsiness as a diagnostic feature of Asperger syndrome. *Journal of Autism and Developmental Disorders, 22*, 651–656.

Gillberg, C. (2003). Deficits in attention, motor control, and perception: A brief review. *Archives of Disease in Childhood, 88*, 904–910.

Gillberg, C., & Cederlund, M. (2005). Asperger syndrome: Familial and pre- and perinatal factors. *Journal of Autism and Developmental Disorders, 35*, 159–166.

Gillberg, C., Gillberg, C., Rastam, M., & Wentz, E. (2001). The Asperger Syndrome (and High-Functioning Autism)

Diagnostic Interview (ASDI): A preliminary study of a new structured clinical interview. *Autism*, *5*, 57–66.

Golan, O., Baron-Cohen, S., & Hill, J. (2006). The Cambridge Mindreading (CAM) face-voice battery: Testing complex emotion recognition in adults with and without Asperger syndrome. *Journal of Autism and Developmental Disorders, 36*, 169–183.

Grandin, T. (1995). *Thinking in pictures: And other reports from my life with autism*. New York: Doubleday.

Grandin, T. (2001, April). *My mind is a Web browser*. Paper presented at the meeting of More Advanced Individuals with Autism, Asperger's Syndrome, and Pervasive Developmental Disorder (MAAP), Indianapolis, IN.

Grandin, T., & Duffy, K. (2004). *Developing talents: Careers for individuals with Asperger's syndrome and high-functioning autism*. Shawnee Mission, KS: Autism Asperger Publishing.

Gray, C., & White, A. L. (Eds.). (2002). *My social stories book*. New York: Jessica Kingsley.

Green, D., Baird, G., Barnett, A. L., Henderson, L., Huber, J., & Henderson, S. E. (2002). The severity and nature of motor impairment in Asperger's syndrome: A comparison with specific developmental disorder of motor function. *Journal of Child Psychology and Psychiatry, 43*, 655–668.

Griswold, D. E., Barnhill, G. P., Myles, B. S., Hagiwara, T., & Simpson, R. L. (2002). Asperger syndrome and academic achievement. *Focus on Autism and Other Developmental Disabilities, 17*(2), 94–102.

Grossman, J. B., Klin, A., Carter, A. S., & Volkmar, F. R. (2000). Verbal bias in recognition of facial emotions in children with Asperger syndrome. *Journal of Child Psychology and Psychiatry, 41*, 369–379.

Gunter, H. L., Ghaziuddin, M. E., & Ellis, H. D. (2002). Asperger syndrome: Tests of right hemisphere functioning and interhemispheric communication. *Journal of Autism and Developmental Disorders, 32*, 263–281.

Hefter, R. L., Manoach, D. S., & Barton, J. J. S. (2005). Perception of facial expression and facial identity in subjects with social developmental disorders. *Neurology, 65*, 1620–1625.

Hooper, S., Poon, K., Marcus, L., & Fine, C. (2006). Neuropsychological characteristics of school-age children with high-functioning autism: Performance on the NEPSY. *Child Neuropsychology, 12*, 299–305.

Howlin, P. (2000). Assessment instruments for Asperger syndrome. *Child Psychology and Psychiatry Review, 5*, 120–129.

Howlin, P., Alcock, J., & Burkin, C. (2005). An eight-year follow-up of a supported employment service for high ability adults with autism or Asperger syndrome. *Autism, 9*, 533–549.

Hubert, B., Wicker, B., Moore, D., Monfardini, E., Duverger, H., Da Fonséca, D., et al. (in press). Brief report: Recognition of emotional and non-emotional biological motion in individuals with autistic spectrum disorders. *Journal of Autism and Developmental Disorders*.

Hurlbutt, K., & Chalmers, L. (2004). Employment and adults with Asperger syndrome. *Focus on Autism and Other Developmental Disabilities, 19*, 215–222.

Individuals with Disabilities Education Act, 20 U.S.C. § 1401 et seq. (1990).

Individual with Disabilities Education Improvement Act, 34 CFR C.F.R. § 300 and 301 (2006).

J. L., M. L. and K. L. v. Mercer Island School District (W.D. WA 2006).

James, W. (1950). *The principles of psychology* (2 vols.). New York: Dover. (Original work published 1890)

Jensen, P. S., Hinshaw, S. P., & Swanson, J. M. (2001). Findings from the NIMH Multimodal Treatment Study of ADHD (MTA): Implications and applications for primary care providers. *Developmental and Behavioral Pediatrics, 22*, 60–73.

Johnson, D. J., & Mykelbust, H. R. (1967). *Learning disabilities: Educational principals and practices*. New York: Grune & Stratton.

Johnson, S. A. (2004). Social processing in Asperger's disorder. *Dissertation Abstracts International, 64*(7-B), 3552.

Joliffe, T., & Baron-Cohen, S. (1997). Are people with autism and Asperger syndrome faster than normal on the Embedded Figures Test? *Journal of Child Psychology and Psychiatry, 38*, 527–534.

Kadesjo, B., Gillberg, C., & Hagberg, B. (1999). Brief report: Autism and Asperger syndrome in seven-year-old children: A total population study. *Journal of Autism and Developmental Disorders, 29*, 327–331.

Kaland, N., Moller-Nielsen, A., Callesen, K., Mortensen, E. L., Gottlieb, D., & Smith, L. (2002). New "advanced" test of theory of mind: Evidence of children and adolescents with Asperger's syndrome. *Journal of Child Psychology and Psychiatry, 43*, 517–528.

Kanner, L. (1943). Autistic disturbances of affective contact. *Nervous Child, 2*, 217–250.

Kanner, L., & Eisenberg, L. (1956). Early infantile autism 1943–1955. *American Journal of Orthopsychiatry, 26*, 55–65.

Kasari, C., & Rotheram-Fuller, E. (2005). Current trends in psychological research on children with high-functioning autism and Asperger disorder. *Current Opinion in Psychiatry, 18*, 497–501.

Kiker, K. M. (2006). A clinician's guide to social skills groups for children and adolescents with Asperger's syndrome. *Dissertation Abstracts International, 66*(8-B), 4486B.

Klin, A., Jones, W., Schultz, R., Volkmar, F., & Cohen, D. (2002). Visual fixation patterns during viewing of naturalistic social situations as predictors of social competence in individuals with autism. *Archives of General Psychiatry, 59*, 809–816.

Klin, A., Pauls, D., Schultz, R., & Volkmar, F. (2005). Three diagnostic approaches to Asperger syndrome: Implications for research. *Journal of Autism and Developmental Disorders, 35*, 221–234.

Klin, A., Saulnier, C. A., Sparrow, S. S., Cicchetti, D. V., Volkmar, F. R., & Lord, C. (in press). Social and communication abilities and disabilities in higher functioning individuals with autism spectrum disorders. *Journal of Autism and Developmental Disorders*.

Klin, A., Volkmar, F. R., & Sparrow, S. S. (2000). *Asperger syndrome*. New York: Guilford.

Kranowitz, C., & Miller, L. (2005). *The out of sync child*. New York: Berkeley Publishing Group.

Lauritsen, M. B., Pedersen, C. B., & Mortensen, P. B. (2004). The incidence and prevalence of pervasive developmental disorders: A Danish population-based study. *Psychological Medicine, 34*, 1339–1346.

Lee, D. O., & Ousley, O. Y. (2006). Attention-Deficit Hyperactivity Disorder symptoms in a clinic sample of children and adolescents with pervasive developmental disorders. *Journal of Child and Adolescent Psychopharmacology, 16*, 737–746.

Little, L. (2002). Middle-class mothers' perceptions of peer and sibling victimization among children with Asperger's syndrome and nonverbal learning disorders. *Issues in Comprehensive Pediatric Nursing, 25*, 43–57.

Magnusen, C. L., & Attwood, T. (2005). *Teaching children with autism and related spectrum disorders: An art and a science.* Philadelphia: Jessica Kingsley.

Marks, S. U., Schrader, C., Levine, M., Hagie, C., Longaker, T., Morales, M., et al. (1999). Social skills for social ills: Supporting the social skills development of adolescents with Asperger's syndrome. *Teaching Exceptional Children, 32*(2), 56–61.

Marriage, K. J., Gordon, V., & Brand, L. (1995). A social skills group for boys with Asperger's syndrome. *Australian and New Zealand Journal of Psychiatry, 29*, 58–62.

Marston, G. M., & Clarke, D. J. (1999). Making contact: Bereavement and Asperger's syndrome. *Irish Journal of Psychological Medicine, 16*, 29–31.

McConachie, H., Le Couteur, A., & Honey, E. (2005). Can a diagnosis of Asperger syndrome be made in very young children with suspected autism spectrum disorder? *Journal of Autism and Developmental Disorders, 35*, 167–176.

McLaughlin-Cheng, E. (1998). Asperger syndrome and autism: A literature review and meta-analysis. *Focus on Autism and Other Developmental Disabilities, 13*, 234–245.

Meyer, R. N., & Attwood, T. (2001). *Asperger syndrome employment workbook: An employment workbook for adults with Asperger syndrome.* Philadelphia: Jessica Kingsley.

Morton, O. (2001, December). Think different? Autism researcher Simon Baron-Cohen on "mindblind" engineers, hidden pictures, and a future designed for people with Asperger's [Electronic version]. *Wired, 9*. Retrieved February 19, 2007, from http://www.wired.com/wired/archive/9.12/baron-cohen.html

Mottron, L. (2004). Matching strategies in cognitive research with individuals with high-functioning autism: Current practices, instrument biases, and recommendations. *Journal of Autism and Developmental Disorders, 34*, 19–27.

Moyes, R. A. (2002). *Addressing the challenging behavior of children with high-functioning autism/Asperger syndrome in the classroom: A guide for teachers and parents*. Philadelphia: Jessica Kingsley.

Musarra, N. L. (2006). Information-processing skills related to working memory in individuals with Asperger's disorder. *Dissertation Abstracts International, 66*(8-B), 4494.

Myles, B. S., & Adreon, D. (2001). *Asperger syndrome and adolescence: Practical solutions for school success*. Shawnee Mission, KS: Autism Asperger Publishing.

Myles, B. S., Hagiwara, T., Dunn, W., Rinner, L. Reese, M., Huggins, A., et al. (2004). Sensory issues in children with Asperger syndrome and autism. *Education and Training in Developmental Disabilities, 39*, 283–290.

Myles, B. S., & Simpson, R. L. (1998). *Asperger syndrome: A guide for educators and parents*. Austin, TX: PRO-ED.

Myles, B. S., & Southwick, J. (1999). *Asperger syndrome and difficult moments: Practical solutions for tantrums, rage, and meltdowns*. Shawnee Mission, KS: Autism Asperger Publishing.

Nash, J. M. (2002, May 6). The secrets of autism [Electronic version]. *Time*. Retrieved February 19, 2007, from http://www.time.com/time/magazine/article/0,9171,1002364-1,00.html

Nesbitt, S. (2000). Why and why not? Factors influencing employment for adults with Asperger's syndrome. *Autism, 4*, 357–369.

Neu, T. W., & Weinfeld, R. (2006). *Helping boys succeed in school: A practical guide for parents and teachers*. Waco, TX: Prufrock Press.

Ozonoff, S., Garcia, N., Clark, E., & Lainhart, J. (2005). MMPI-2 personality profiles of high-functioning adults with autism spectrum disorders. *Assessment, 12*, 86–95.

Ozonoff, S., South, M., & Miller, J. N. (2000). DSM-IV-defined Asperger syndrome: Cognitive, behavioral and early history differentiation from high-functioning autism. *Autism, 4*, 29–46.

Palmer, A. (2006). *Realizing the college dream with autism or Asperger syndrome: A parent's guide to student success*. New York: Jessica Kingsley.

Pfeiffer, E. A. (2004). Sensory modulation and affective disorders in children and adolescents with Asperger syndrome. *Dissertation Abstracts International, 64*(7-B), 3231.

Pierce, K., & Courchesne, E. (2000). Exploring the neurofunctional organization of face processing in autism. *Archives of General Psychiatry, 57*, 344–346.

Powers, M. D., & Poland, J. (2003). *Asperger syndrome and your child: A parent's guide*. New York: HarperCollins.

Ralabate, P. (Ed.). (2006). *The puzzle of autism*. Washington, DC: National Education Association. Retrieved April 27, 2006, http://www.nea.org/specialed/images/autismpuzzle.pdf

Raja, M., & Azzoni, A. (2001). Asperger's disorder in the emergency psychiatric setting. *General Hospital Psychiatry, 23*, 285–293.

Rinehart, N. J., Bradshaw, J. L., Brereton, A. V., & Tonge, B. J. (2001). Movement preparation in high-functioning autism and Asperger disorder: A serial choice reaction time task involving motor reprogramming. *Journal of Autism and Developmental Disorders, 31*, 79–88.

Rogers, S. (2000). Interventions that facilitate socialization in children with autism. *Journal of Autism and Developmental Disorders, 30*, 399–409.

Rourke, B. P. (1989). *Nonverbal learning disabilities: The syndrome and the model.* New York: Guilford.

Rourke, B. P., & Tsatsanis, K. D. (2000). Nonverbal learning disabilities. In A. Klin, F. R. Volkmar, and S. S. Sparrow (Eds.), *Asperger syndrome* (pp. 231–253). New York: Guilford.

Russell, E., & Sofronoff, K. (2005). Anxiety and social worries in children with Asperger syndrome. *Australian and New Zealand Journal of Psychiatry, 39*, 633–638.

Safran, S. P. (2001). Asperger syndrome: The emerging challenge to special education. *Exceptional Children, 67*, 151–160.

Sattler, J. M. (2001). *Assessment of children: Cognitive applications* (4th ed.). La Mesa, CA: Author.

Schatz, A. M., Weimer, A. K., & Trauner, D. A. (2002). Brief report: Attention differences in Asperger syndrome. *Journal of Autism and Developmental Disorders, 32*, 333–336.

Schultz, R. T., Gauthier, I., Klin, A., Fulbright, R. K., Anderson, A.W., Volkmar, F., et al. (2000). Abnormal ventral temporal cortical activity during face discrimination among individuals with autism and Asperger syndrome. *Archives of General Psychiatry, 57*, 331–340.

Shah, A., & Frith, U. (1983). An islet of ability in autistic children: A research note. *Journal of Child Psychology and Psychiatry, 24*, 613–620.

Shapiro, D. (2006, August). *ADHD review.* Lecture presented at Siena School, Silver Spring, MD.

Silver, M., & Oakes, P. (2001). Evaluation of a new computer intervention to teach people with autism or Asperger syndrome to recognize and predict emotions in others. *Autism, 5*, 299–316.

Sofronoff, K., Leslie, A., & Brown, W. (2004). Parent management training and Asperger syndrome: A randomized controlled trial to evaluate a parent based intervention. *Autism, 8*, 301–317.

Solomon, M., Goodlin-Jones, B. L., & Anders, T. F. (2004). A social adjustment enhancement intervention for high functioning autism, Asperger's syndrome, and pervasive developmental disorder NOS. *Journal of Autism and Developmental Disorders, 34*, 649–668.

Suckling, A., & Temple, C. (2001). *Bullying: A whole-school approach*. Philadelphia: Jessica Kingsley.

Szatmari, P. (2000). The classification of autism, Asperger's syndrome, and pervasive developmental disorder. *Canadian Journal of Psychiatry, 45*, 731–738.

Szatmari, P., Brenner, R., & Nagy, J. (1989). Asperger's syndrome: A review of clinical features. *Canadian Journal of Psychiatry, 34*, 554–560.

Tanaka, J. W., Lincoln, S., & Hegg, L. (2003). A framework for the study and treatment of face processing deficits in autism. In G. Schwarzer & H. Leder (Eds.), *The development of face processing* (pp. 101–119). Berlin, Germany: Hogrefe & Huber.

Tani, P., Lindberg, N., Appelberg, B., Nieminen-von Wendt, T., von Wendt, L., & Porkka-Heiskanen, T. (2006). Childhood inattention and hyperactivity symptoms self-reported by adults with Asperger syndrome. *Psychopathology, 39*, 49–54.

Tantam, D. (2000). Psychological disorder in adolescents and adults with Asperger syndrome. *Autism, 4*, 47–62.

Teitelbaum, O., Benton, T., Shah, P. K., Prince, A., Kelly, J. L., & Teitelbaum, P. (2004). Eshkol-Wachman movement notation in diagnosis: The early detection of Asperger's syndrome. *Proceedings of the National Academy of Sciences of the United States of America, 101*, 11909–11914.

Tomlinson, C. A. (1999). *The differentiated classroom: Responding to the needs of all learners.* Alexandria, VA: Association for Supervision and Curriculum Development.

Volkmar, F. R., & Klin, A. (1998). Asperger syndrome and nonverbal learning disabilities. In E. Schopler, G. B. Mesibov, & L. J. Kunce (Eds.), *Asperger syndrome or high-functioning autism?* (pp. 107–121). New York: Plenum Press.

Walker, D. R., Thompson, A., Zwaigenbaum, L., Goldberg, J., Bryson, S. E., Mahoney, W. J., et al. (2004). Specifying PDD-NOS: A comparison of PDD-NOS, Asperger syndrome, and autism. *Journal of the American Academy of Child and Adolescent Psychiatry, 43*, 172–180.

Weinfeld, R., Barnes-Robinson, L., Jeweler, S., & Roffman Shevitz, B. (2006). *Smart kids with learning difficulties: Overcoming obstacles and realizing potential.* Waco, TX: Prufrock Press.

White, S., Hill, E., Winston, J., & Frith, U. (2006). An islet of social ability in Asperger syndrome: Judging social attributes from faces. *Brain and Cognition, 61*, 69–77.

Williams, E. (2004). Who really needs "theory" of mind? An interpretative phenomenological analysis of the autobiographical writings of ten high-functioning individuals with an autism spectrum disorder. *Theory & Psychology, 14*, 704–724.

Williams, M. S., & Shellenberger, S. (1996). *How does your engine run? A leader's guide to the alert program for self-regulation.* Albuquerque, NM: Therapyworks.

Wing, L. (1981). Asperger's syndrome: A clinical account. *Psychological Medicine, 11*, 115–129.

Woodbury-Smith, M. R., Robinson, J., Wheelwright, S., & Baron-Cohen, S. (2005). Screening adults for Asperger syndrome using the AQ: A preliminary study of its diagnostic validity in clinical practice. *Journal of Autism and Developmental Disorders, 35*, 331–335.

World Health Organization. (2006). *International statistical classification of diseases and related health problems* (10th revision). Washington, DC: Author.

Wymbs, B. T., Robb, J. A., Chronis, A. M., Massetti, G. M., Fabiano, G. A., Arnold, F. W., et al. (2005). Long-term, multimodal treatment of a child with Asperger's syndrome and comorbid disruptive behavior problems: A case illustration. *Cognitive and Behavioral Practice, 12*, 338–350.

Ylisaukko-oja, T., Nieminen-von Wendt, T., Kempas, E., Sarenius, S., Varilo, T., von Wendt, L., et al. (2004). Genome-wide scan for loci of Asperger syndrome. *Molecular Psychiatry, 9*, 161–168.

Appendix A

Resources

National Organizations

ASPEN

9 Aspen Circle
Edison, NJ 08820
Phone: (732) 321-0880
E-mail: info@AspenNJ.org
Web site: http://www.aspennj.org

Asperger's Association of New England (AANE)

182 Main Street
Watertown, MA 02472
Phone: (617) 393-3824
E-mail: info@aane.org
Web site: http://aane.autistics.org

Autism Network International (ANI)

P.O. Box 35448
Syracuse, NY 13235-5448
E-mail: jisincla@mailbox.syr.edu
Web site: http://ani.autistics.org

Autism Research Institute (ARI)

4182 Adams Avenue
San Diego, CA 92116
Phone: (619) 281-7165
Web site: http://www.autismwebsite.com/ari

Autism Resource Network

904 Mainstreet #100
Hopkins, MN 55343
Phone (952) 988-0088
E-mail: info@autismshop.com
Web site: http://www.autismshop.com

Autism Society of America (ASA)

7910 Woodmont Ave., Ste. 300
Bethesda, MD 20814-3067
Phone: (301) 657-0881
Web site: http://www.autism-society.org

Autism Society of North Carolina

505 Oberlin Road, Ste. 230
Raleigh, NC 27605-1345
Phone: (919) 743-0204
E-mail: info@autismsociety-nc.org
Web site: http://www.autismsociety-nc.org

Autism Speaks

2 Park Ave., 11th Floor
New York, NY 10016
Phone: (212) 252-8584
E-mail: contactus@autismspeaks.org
Web site: http://www.autismspeaks.org

Council For Exceptional Children

1110 North Glebe Road, Ste. 300
Arlington, VA 22201
Phone: (703) 620-3660; (888) 232-7733
Web site: http://www.cec.sped.org

Cure Autism Now

5455 Wilshire Blvd., Ste. 2250
Los Angeles, CA 90036-4272
Phone: (323) 549-0500; (888) 828-8476
E-mail: info@cureautismnow.org
Web site: http://www.cureautismnow.org

Future Horizons

721 W. Abram Street
Arlington, TX 76013
Phone: (800) 489-0727
Web site: http://www.FHautism.com

Kennedy Krieger Institute

707 North Broadway
Baltimore, MD 21205
Phone: (800) 873-3377
E-mail: info@kennedykrieger.org
Web site: http://www.kennedykrieger.org

Learning Disabilities Association of America (LDA)

4156 Library Road
Pittsburgh, PA 15234-1349
Phone: (412) 341-1515
Web site: http://www.ldanatl.org

MAAP Services for Autism & Asperger Syndrome

P.O. Box 524
Crown Point, IN 46308
Phone: (219) 662-1311
E-mail: info@maapservices.org
Web site: http://www.asperger.org

M.I.N.D. Institute

2825 50th Street
Sacramento, CA 95817
Phone: (888) 883-0961
Web site: http://www.ucdmc.ucdavis.edu/mindinstitute

National Autism Center

41 Pacella Park Drive
Randolph, MA 02368
Phone: (877) 313-3833
E-mail: info@nationalautismcenter.org
Web site: http://www.nationalautismcenter.org

National Information Center for Children with Disabilities (NICHCY)

P.O. Box 1492
Washington, DC 20013
Phone: (800) 695-0285
E-mail: nichcy@aed.org
Web site: http://www.nichcy.org

National Institute of Mental Health (NIMH)

6001 Executive Blvd., Rm. 8184, MSC 9663
Bethesda, MD 20892-9663
Phone: (866) 615-6464
E-mail: nimhinfo@nih.gov
Web site: http://www.nimh.nih.gov

Unlocking Autism

P.O. Box 15388
Baton Rouge, LA 70895
Phone: (866) 366-3361
Web site: www.unlockingautism.org

Yale University Child Study Center

230 South Frontage Rd.
New Haven, CT 06520
Phone: (203) 785-2513
Web site: http://childstudycenter.yale.edu

Web Sites

Asperger Info.com
http://www.aspergerinfo.com

Asperger Planet
http://www.aspergerplanet.com

Autism Link
http://www.autismlink.com

Asperger's Disorder Homepage
http://www.aspergers.com

Attacking Asperger's Syndrome
http://www.linktoaustin.com/as

Autism Resources Page
http://www.autism-resources.com

Center for the Study of Autism
http://www.autism.org

Education Law Center
http://www.edlawcenter.org

The Global and Regional Asperger Syndrome Partnership (GRASP)
http://www.grasp.org

K–12 Academics
http://k12academics.com/aspergers.htm

National Center to Improve Practice in Special Education Through Technology, Media and Materials (NCIP)
http://www2.edc.org/NCIP

OASIS—Online Asperger Syndrome Information and Support
http://www.aspergersyndrome.org

Tony Attwood's Web Site
http://www.tonyattwood.com.au

University of Michigan Health System Autism and Pervasive Developmental Disorders
http://www.med.umich.edu/1libr/yourchild/autism.htm

U.S. Department of Education
http://www.ed.gov

Wrightslaw
http://www.wrightslaw.com

Wrong Planet
http://www.wrongplanet.net

Appendix B

Checklist of Issues That Teachers and Parents May Observe in the Classroom

Parents and teachers should utilize this checklist to note issues that they are observing in the classroom for students with AS. It can serve as a discussion tool for parent-teacher conferences and 504/IEP meetings.

- ❏ Problems with social interactions
- ❏ Very focused areas of interest and expertise
- ❏ Need for predictability
- ❏ Problems with language
- ❏ Problems with abstract reasoning
- ❏ Problems with sensory hyper- or hyposensitivity
- ❏ Problems with anxiety, depression, and emotional regulation
- ❏ Problems with attention, organization, and other areas of executive functioning
- ❏ Problems with motor issues including written production
- ❏ Problems with ritualistic, repetitive, or rigid behavior

Appendix C

Intervention Plan for Students With AS

Teachers and school staff members should use this tool as a way to formulate a school plan for students with AS. Fill out Parts 1–3 to analyze what is currently happening with the student and then fill out Parts 4 and 5 to plan what needs to be done.

Name:

Date:

School:

1. **Evidence of Strengths:**

   Test scores:

   Performance in school (When does the student show interest, perseverance, self-regulation, and outstanding achievement?):

   Performance in the community:

2. Evidence of Learning Challenges:

Problems with social interactions:

Very focused areas of interest and expertise:

Need for predictability:

Problems with language:

Problems with abstract reasoning:

Problems with sensory hyper- or hyposensitivity:

Problems with anxiety, depression, and emotional regulation:

Problems with attention, organization, and other areas of executive functioning:

Problems with motor issues including written production:

Problems with ritualistic, repetitive, or rigid behavior:

3. Current Program:

Instruction in the area of strengths (gifted or advanced-level instruction):

Adaptations:

Accommodations:

Special instruction in areas that are affected by the disability:

Problems with social interactions:

Very focused areas of interest and expertise:

Need for predictability:

Problems with language:

Problems with abstract reasoning:

Problems with sensory hyper- or hyposensitivity:

Problems with anxiety, depression, and emotional regulation:

Problems with attention, organization, and other areas of executive functioning:

Problems with motor issues including written production:

Problems with ritualistic, repetitive, or rigid behavior:

Behavior/Attention management:

Counseling (in school, group therapy):

Case management (communication between home and school and among staff):

4. Recommendations:

Strength-based instruction:

Adaptations:

Accommodations:

Special instruction in the areas affected by the disability:

Problems with social interactions:

Very focused areas of interest and expertise:

Need for predictability:

Problems with language:

Problems with abstract reasoning:

Problems with sensory hyper- or hyposensitivity:

Problems with anxiety, depression, and emotional regulation:

Problems with attention, organization, and other areas of executive functioning:

Problems with motor issues including written production:

Problems with ritualistic, repetitive, or rigid behavior:

Behavior/Attention management:

Counseling:

Case management:

5. Next steps:

Note. Adapted from *Smart Kids With Learning Difficulties: Overcoming Obstacles and Realizing Potential* (pp. 168-170), by R. Weinfeld, L. Barnes-Robinson, S. Jeweler, and B. Roffman Shevitz, 2006, Waco, TX: Prufrock Press. Copyright © 2006 Prufrock Press.

Appendix D

Quick Reference to Problem Areas and Interventions

Strategies and Interventions That Work With Social Interactions

Protect students from bullying and teasing.

Educate other students about AS and about the child's unique strengths and challenges.

Utilize strengths and interests in cooperative learning.

Teach theory of mind: Learning to understand the perspectives, feelings, and thoughts of others.

Teach students how to read and react to nonverbal social cues.

Teach students how to participate in conversations.

Teach students to identify and understand emotions.

Strategies and Interventions That Work With Very Focused Areas of Interest and Expertise

Provide a specific time of the day for focus on the area of interest.

Help students develop their area of interest and relate it to future employment.

Use the special area of interest as a bridge to other topics.

Use the area of interest as a way to facilitate social interaction.

Use the student's area of interest to help regulate behavior.

Strategies and Interventions That Work to Provide Predictability

Provide clear rules and consequences.

Provide clear physical structure in the classroom.

Provide a clear physical schedule in the classroom.

Prepare for changes and transitions.

Provide structure for unstructured time.

Provide instruction about the hidden curriculum.

Strategies and Interventions That Work for Problems With Language

Avoid or carefully explain ambiguous language such as idioms, metaphors, and figures of speech.

Avoid or explain the use of sarcasm or jokes with double meanings.

Avoid or explain the use of nicknames.

Teach students how to find key words and concepts in directions and instructions.

Strategies or Interventions That Work to Improve Abstract Reasoning

Break down the goal of the lesson into its component parts and provide supports.

Utilize "naturalistic" instruction.

Provide appropriate accommodations throughout instruction.

Provide adaptations to the way the lesson will be taught.

Provide explicit instruction to ensure understanding of the concept being taught.

Move from specifics to generalizations.

Provide alternative ways for students to demonstrate understanding that allow them to utilize their strengths.

Strategies or Interventions That Work to Deal With Hyper- and Hyposensitivity

Alter or change the environment to decrease factors to which the student may be hyper- or hyposensitive.

Work proactively to prepare the student to deal with his issues around hyper- or hyposensitivity.

Employ strategies that serve to help the students to calm themselves.

Strategies or Interventions That Work With Anxiety, Depression, and Emotional Regulation

Work to proactively minimize situations that will cause emotional problems.

Identify signs of stress and/or overstimulation early and intervene before the problem becomes overwhelming.

Allow and encourage students to employ techniques that will allow for self calming and regaining emotional control.

Allow students to move to a special area in the classroom or building.

Help students to gain skills in monitoring and responding to their own behavior.

Teach students to prepare for stressful, overstimulating, and uncomfortable situations.

Consider medication with a psychiatrist or pediatrician and behavioral consultation with a psychologist or behavior specialist.

Strategies or Interventions That Work to Improve Attention, Organization, and Other Areas of Executive Functioning

Use visual schedules.

Use proximity to and prompting from the teacher.

Structure work periods.

Structure the environment.

Teach students to monitor their own attention.

Use visual supports that aide with completion of assignments.

Support organization with rubrics, study guides, and outlines.

Provide classroom structures that support organization of materials.

Utilize technology.

Provide systematic supports for organizational help.

Structure time during the school day for organization of assignments and materials.

Strategies and Interventions That Work to Deal With Motor Issues Including Written Production

Provide support with and alternatives to physical education and recess.

Support in acquiring written language skills.

Provide tools that allow for improvement of handwriting.

Provide alternatives that allow students to write more easily or to circumvent writing.

Allow and encourage students to use technology as an alternative to handwriting.

Strategies and Interventions That Work to Deal With Ritualistic, Repetitive, or Rigid Behavior

Develop a Functional Behavioral Analysis (FBA).

If possible, intervene before the behavior becomes a habit, distracting, or disruptive.

Respond to behaviors in a way that will help minimize the impact of the behavior and/or extinguish it.

Appendix E

Program Options for Students With AS

Parents and teachers can utilize this checklist for gathering information about the educational options available for a student with AS.

❑ Instruction in regular classes

Options:____

____

❑ Instruction in special classes

Options:____

____

❑ Special schools

Options:____

____

❑ Alternative school programs

Options:____

____

❑ Homeschooling

Options:____

____

❑ Home and hospital teaching

Options:____

____

Appendix F

The following are specific strategies for dealing with attention problems and ADHD.

For the Classroom Teacher

- Be prepared to refocus or recue students frequently.
- Be prepared to repeat rules and instructions.
- Repeat explanations of consequences for both positive and negative behavior choices.
- Use immediate consequences (praise, rewards, privileges) for task completion as appropriate.
- Employ activities and consequences of high interest to the student.
- Start incentives before punishments in the management program.
- Strive for consistency in expectations for the child and all significant adults' responses to him.
- Anticipate problem situations and activities.
- Develop realistic expectations for what he can and cannot be held accountable for in developing goals for his behavior.
- Practice forgiveness.
- Coordinate all management techniques in school with parents in an integrated fashion, so that the same rules apply and receive follow-up in all situations.
- It is suggested that a contract system might be employed to be sure that the child is keeping track of his assignments. Parents should sign off daily on a contract outlining appro-

priate consequences and special privileges for degrees of completion.

- Select one person at school to coordinate communications between school and the parents in order to maintain consistency.
- The child may benefit from external cues or calming techniques to focus on the whole message being delivered and for the relevant cues to be considered. A consistent gesture or signal for all of the child's teachers to use in regaining her attention should be developed and practiced.
- Highly structured routines and specific instructions should be implemented.
- Peripheral stimulation can be distracting. The child could be seated in such a way that distracting influences are minimized. He should not be placed in the back of the room or next to the window where he will constantly be subjected to distracting influences. Usually, a seat near the front of the room close to the teacher will help him maintain attention.
- Be sure to keep unnecessary materials off of the student's desk. Extraneous materials should be put away immediately after use.
- Explicit directions for each step of the learning process must be indicated clearly. Short tasks with a clear end in sight and a reinforcement for each step of the learning process are effective ways of helping students complete lengthy assignments.
- Utilize time-out if necessary.
- Allow the child to have passes to permit interruptions. Reward unused interruption passes.
- Use a visual focal point on the blackboard or the teacher's hand, to form a habitual place for the child to refocus.
- Use a brief relaxation, meditation, or quiet calming activity to allow the student to recenter himself.

- It is also sometimes effective to permit a "squeeze ball" or other unobtrusive and safe manipulative to keep hands busy when they are temporarily idle.
- Identify one or more areas of strength, talent, and interest to build self-esteem and confidence.
- Don't leave your class unattended.
- Prioritize multiple tasks.
- Develop a timeline for long-term projects.
- Utilize study guides, outlines, and charts for following progress.
- Ensure in class that homework assignments have been noted and understood before leaving for the day.
- Break down large tasks into smaller clear chunks, which can be reviewed and monitored sequentially.
- For nonroutine tasks, develop a simple calendar and "to do" list. For routine tasks, utilize a daily responsibilities list with clear consequences for compliance/noncompliance.
- Keep an envelope for important papers attached to his school notebook to be checked regularly by his parents.

For Parents

- A physician who is able to consider possible pharmacological interventions and monitor the medicine's effectiveness should see the child regularly.
- A program of home and school management should be employed including the use of contracts, natural consequences for behavior, and other techniques.
- The student can frequently gain improvement from counseling to help him explore his feelings and reactions to his atten-

tion needs, to explore their implications and the adjustments to be expected with medications or other interventions, and to act as an advocate for himself in requiring appropriate accommodations.

- Therapeutic consultation for the child's parents is suggested so that they may be able to work together in developing and sustaining a shared, effective management plan.
- The child can gain from social skills groups and/or summer camps available for students with similar needs.
- Use a phone network of classmates to check on assignments as necessary.

About the Authors

Stephan M. Silverman, Ph.D., is a highly regarded child/adolescent psychological diagnostician with more than 30 years of experience. He currently specializes in the assessment and education of students with autistic spectrum disorder. Stephan acts as a liaison psychologist to several schools in the Washington, DC, area, specializing in Asperger's syndrome.

Rich Weinfeld is a national leader in the education of smart children with learning difficulties. Weinfeld was instrumental in coordinating the Montgomery County, MD, gifted and learning-disabled program and is currently an educational advocate in the Washington, DC, metropolitan area. He is the author of two previous books, *Smart Kids With Learning Difficulties* and *Helping Boys Succeed in School*. To learn more about Weinfeld, please visit http://www.richweinfeld.com.